Life Hacks

Safe Products and Easy Cleaning Methods

(Life-changing Strategies to Improve Executive Functioning)

William Yates

Published By **Ryan Princeton**

William Yates

All Rights Reserved

Life Hacks: Safe Products and Easy Cleaning Methods (Life-changing Strategies to Improve Executive Functioning)

ISBN 978-1-77485-512-6

No part of this guidebook shall be reproduced in any form without permission in writing from the publisher except in the case of brief quotations embodied in critical articles or reviews.

Legal & Disclaimer

The information contained in this ebook is not designed to replace or take the place of any form of medicine or professional medical advice. The information in this ebook has been provided for educational & entertainment purposes only.

The information contained in this book has been compiled from sources deemed reliable, and it is accurate to the best of the Author's knowledge; however, the Author cannot guarantee its accuracy and validity and cannot be held liable for any errors or omissions. Changes are periodically made to this book. You must consult your doctor or get professional medical advice before using any of the suggested remedies, techniques, or information in this book.

Upon using the information contained in this book, you agree to hold harmless the Author from and against any damages, costs, and expenses, including any legal fees potentially resulting from the application of any of the information provided by this guide. This disclaimer applies to any damages or injury caused by the use and application, whether directly or indirectly, of any advice or information presented, whether for breach of contract, tort, negligence, personal injury, criminal intent, or under any other cause of action.

You agree to accept all risks of using the information presented inside this book. You need to consult a professional medical practitioner in order to ensure you are both able and healthy enough to participate in this program.

Table of Contents

INTRODUCTION 1

CHAPTER 1: LIFE HACKS FOR YOUR HOME 6

CHAPTER 2: LIFE HACKS FOR YOUR OFFICE 25

CHAPTER 3: REDUCING STRESSS AND INCREASING PRODUCTIVITY 30

CHAPTER 4: TRAVEL HACKS 37

CHAPTER 5: MEMORY HACKS 44

CHAPTER 6: 17 ONLINE HACKS TO SAVE MONEY AND MAKE MORE 51

CHAPTER 7: 23 SIMPLE HACKS TO SAVE MONEY WHEN VISITING STORES, THEATER HOTELS,, RESTAURANTS 65

CHAPTER 8: 7 HACKS TO HELP YOU GET THE BEST OUT OF YOUR COLLEGE ENVIRONMENT 83

CHAPTER 9: 10 TECHNIQUES TO GET A JOB AND MANIPULATE THE WORK ENVIRONMENT TO YOUR ADVANTAGE 89

CHAPTER 10: GENERAL LIFE HACKS TO GET THE BEST OUT OF LIFE 97

CHAPTER 11: HOW TO BUILD YOUR ENERGY 126

CONCLUSION 183

INTRODUCTION

"We are unable to solve our issues using the same way of thinking that spawned them."

-- Albert Einstein

In the course of your daily life you are likely you'll encounter issues which can cause inconvenience for you. Whatever your situation you are, your life will surely discover ways to make your life stress-inducing. Stress can be triggered by numerous sources. From something as basic as taking the odor off of your clothes, to something as crucial as working more efficiently.

Don't let these small problems to ruin your day! It is easy to solve problems and challenges by mastering how to live your life! Life hacks can enable you to handle minor issues and stress in a the most graceful manner. They will make your life more easy and comfortable.

What are the life tips?

"Life hack" or "life hack" was first coined by computer specialists in the early 1980's in reference to methods to speed up the flow of work. The term "life hack can refer to any shortcut or trick which can make everyday tasks more productive and efficient.

There are a variety of low-cost strategies and tips that will help make your life a bit easier and more comfortable. They're simple to follow. Even the most chaotic person on earth can easily use life hacks to resolve issues and difficulties.

Are you concerned that you're spending too long trying to manage and get rid of clutter? Do you wish to have an efficient home? When you employ life hacks, you'll not just save time, but also reduce your expenses! Understanding how to apply life hacks can simplify your life and make it a more simple. You'll definitely be more efficient and efficient when you have these tips and tricks.

The majority of us are people of habit. That means that a majority of us are prone to sticking with one method or approach even though it's not necessarily the most effective method of doing things. Life hacks can help you to think outside of the box and accomplish things more efficiently and efficient manner. If you utilize life hacks, it will help you be able to focus on specifics, which can help you complete a task and more enjoyable.

Sometimes, the solutions to all your questions are right there in front of your eyes. It's just a matter of looking at the world that surround you in a different way. You'll see that you can utilize items for other purposes beyond what they were intended to serve. Straws can be used as containers. You can also use the condiments to clean. You can make garbage useful. Imagine the time and money you'll save when you are aware of life hacks that can solve issues you face.

These tips can also aid you in tackling daily problems that arise at your home, at work or even while on the road! These are easy solutions to difficult issues. We've put together some incredible life hacks that can simplify your life. We hope these hacks techniques, tips, and tricks will make things easier that you encounter in your daily routine.

If you find yourself in a situation that is difficult All you need to do is approach the problem as an engineer. People with a lot of experience will grasp the concept behind life hacks. It's about seeing things old in a fresh way.

For some finding new ways to solve problems isn't a natural thing to do. The different life hacks that are available on the internet can aid you in coming up with concepts. It can be difficult to make sense on the final outcome initially, but eventually you'll get grasp of it.

These are easy and trouble free ways to modify and enhance your life and your lifestyle. It is not necessary to be knowledgeable of the science behind this to accomplish it. Life hacks aren't rocket science. Actually, it's straightforward and easy to implement. When you consider some of the strategies are available to your situation, you'll wonder what you could have done to come up with these solutions before!

It is possible to decorate your home in a specific manner, or you may discover an innovative use for an unutilized object, and your living room could be worthy of praise the next time you invite guests over.

You can find it extremely easy to find different life hacks online. People are constantly developing new and innovative ways to help make their lives more convenient.

To get you to grips with life hacks, here are a few suggestions that can inspire you to get involved. These are very easy and you can carry out the majority of these tricks on your own. Actually, the majority of the items you'll require are in your home.

This book you'll learn about life hacks you can apply at the office, at home or when traveling, or even when trying to keep track of things. It is possible to use these techniques in all aspects that you are in!

CHAPTER 1: LIFE HACKS FOR YOUR HOME

Most of the time there are plenty of things to do to be doing when you get home from work. The list of tasks to be done doesn't seem to get done. When you return from job, you'll probably prefer your time to relax over the task of completing household chores and chores. But, if you're doing this frequently the house will be an enormous mess!

After a long day of work it's nearly impossible to summon the motivation to ensure that your house is neat and tidy. With determination and the aid in lifehacks you'll be able to effortlessly complete your chores in no time. If you're familiar with the techniques and techniques of life hacks that you can easily follow, you'll finish your work without wasting your energy.

Imagine how much easier your life will be if you were more efficient with doing the chores of cleaning and laundry. You'll have time to focus on the things you would like to accomplish. Additionally you will have more time with your loved ones.

There are a lot of ways to improve your life that you can applied to your home. There are techniques that can be useful in your living space and kitchen, laundry room bathroom, bedroom or the front yard, as well as your backyard and garage. Anywhere you apply these tricks and tricks, you'll get fantastic results to organize and clean more effectively. The solution to your problem is right at your fingertips!

So what's next? Hacks you can use at home. Here are a few quick suggestions to help make your life easier and manageable.

Life Hacks for your Living Room

Your living room must appear attractive since this is where you'll entertain guests and guests. Here are some suggestions to assist you in being proud of your living space.

As time passes your walls may begin to smell like cigarettes, food or the smell of an "old home." The issue can become more serious when you own pets. It's not easy to eliminate the animal scent when it is stuck on the walls. It isn't necessary to spend thousands of dollars on costly chemicals. Simply clean your furniture and walls with an equal amount of white vinegar, and 8 parts of water to get rid of bad smells from your house.

Carpets look beautiful and classy. However, keeping them takes lots of work. Here are a few tips that can simplify your life.

The furniture you place on your carpet can result in them getting scratch marks. Do not worry about it! Just rub the unsightly areas using a cube of ice. Then, rub with the help of a cloth, and your rug will be as clean as new.

Do you have children or pets that cause your rug to move? To ensure that your carpet or rug in place, you can attach an Velcro strip to the carpet, and then a

Velcro strip to the floor. This trick will ensure that the rug stays in position.

It's a surprise that drinks and food can be used to aid in furniture maintenance. Furniture made of wood is gorgeous, and can give your living space an old-fashioned appearance. But, you must put in extra effort if you would like your furniture to look nice.

It is possible to use flat beer to wash your furniture. All you need do is put the beer onto a clean cloth and then wipe it off the furniture made of wood. This simple procedure will assist in restoring the colour that your furnishings have.

If your furniture is damaged and scratches, you'll discover the most unlikely solution to your issue by using the walnut. Rub a walnut over the surface of your furniture and the walnut oil can bring back the flawless appearance of your furniture made of wood.

Life Hacks to Your Kitchen and Laundry

Cleaning your kitchen and laundry can be among the most demanding tasks you must complete to maintain your home. Here are some suggestions to ease the burden.

For Kitchen-

Cleaning your kitchen can be an overwhelming task. It is necessary to wash your floor, sink as well as all your cabinets. Additionally there is also the need to clean the food and cooking equipment. If you do not employ techniques for life, it can take you a long time to get the kitchen clean. Here are some strategies you can apply for keeping your kitchen neat.

Cleaning your stove isn't easy as it is susceptible to a myriad of spills and messes that stick to it. It isn't necessary to purchase costly solutions to accomplish the task. By using this hack, the task of cleaning your stove is much simpler! Combine 1 tablespoon of salt , baking soda, one tablespoon along with one cup of water. Mix the mixture together. Make the paste as any other cleaner and clean away!

You can easily remove the stains from tea and coffee cups by rub them using lemon peel and salt. This combination can be very effective against stains and dirt.

If you are using blenders or food processor, there is no have to clean and scrub the container. You just need to "blend" or "process" some drops of dishwashing liquid with a half cup of water. Let the machine do the cleaning for you! There is no need to put in effort any longer. All you need to do is hit the button.

Here are some additional ideas to employ in your kitchen.

If your sink is blocked with tablets that dissolve the drains. If you'd like to keep the silverware and glasses from breaking using rubber bands, you can use them to hold them in their place. It is also possible to place old newspapers in the bottom of your trash bin to help absorb juices from leftover food and to keep your trash bins free of dirt and dust. This will keep any type of liquid from causing chaos within your home.

For Laundry

We all love clean and crisp clothing which can provide a professional appearance. But, we all dislike the work required to iron to get the polished appearance. Don't worry about it. Here are some techniques to aid you in getting the task done quicker and more efficient.

The first trick is all you require are aluminum foil. First, take off the ironing protector from the board. After that, just put a piece of foil over the table, then place the protector back onto. Due to the reflection of heat it will be possible to smooth both sides of your clothing in one go. This technique works wonders on clothes made of wool, silk and rayon. If you're traveling be aware that hair straighteners can be used to iron the collars of your Polo shirt.

The smell of clothes could make you feel as if you're wearing something dirty. Food, smoke from cigarettes and sweat may stick onto your shirt which can make you feel like you're unclean. Here are some tips you can apply to make sure that your clothes are free of odors.

Anyone who goes to the gym are aware of how difficult it can be to rid yourself of sweat and body smell. To make it easier for yourself, you can clean your clothing in the gym itself to remove your sweat, odor and sweats as fast as you can. Then wash them in the normal way after you return back home. If the smell is strong then spray white vinegar over the underarms before adding it in the washing machine. Vinegar is among the most potent options you have to fight the smell. This will ensure that your clothes fresh and clean.

If you're trying to eliminate odor in your shoes, the most effective method to accomplish this is to stuff your shoes tea bags. They'll absorb the unpleasant smell you're trying to eliminate.

Clothes require lots of care and attention. You will need to exert more effort to maintain the appearance of your garments. in good condition. Here are some tricks can be used to maintain your clothes looking neat.

If you discover an unexpected ink stain on your clothing just rub it off using hand sanitizer, and then follow up with regular cleaning later. If you find that gum sticks to the shirt of your child's put the shirt into an airtight bag and place it in the freezer. It is very simple to get rid of gum once it's solid. If you wish to hold buttons in place you can simply apply clear nail polish to ensure that they don't fall off.

Tips for a Successful Life in Your Bedroom

Your bedroom ought to be the most relaxing space within your home. It should be a place where you can unwind and be happy with your self after a tiring day of work. This should also be a spot that you are excited to be in. It should be tidy and well-organized to make it easy for you to unwind and rest. Although visitors seldom have access to bedrooms, it doesn't mean that the room should appear like it's been struck by a storm.

Are you looking for ways to tidy your bedroom? Here are some ideas to help you tidy your bedroom in a timely way.

In many bedrooms, space is usually an issue. In most cases there are lots of things and the room appears to be an overflowing chaos. There are bedrooms that have overstuffed furniture. This may cause you to be unable to move about.

If you are trying to arrange your living space, you'll need to consider ways to make the most of space. In most cases rooms can be organized by simply rearranging furniture and maximising space.

You'll be surprised at the extent to which you can make the most of the space you have. For instance walls are not only for posters and pictures. Hang hooks on the walls and utilize them to store bags and purses, scarfs, as well as other accessories.

Do not forget the room behind doors as well. You can hang stuff behind your doors. This is a great place to store items you take right before you leave your home.

We are aware of how difficult it can be to store clothes for various seasons. When you change your clothes and seasons, you need to learn how to make the most space to store those which are not being used. It is possible to store clothes that are not being used under your bed to make the most of space. You can take them out whenever it's time to wear them.

Utilize pockets in your chair to help sort your items. It's ideal for storage of the stationary items and other things you use frequently. The chair can be hung from the pocket to the wall for more convenient access.

Learn how to maximize your closet space also. You'll be amazed to learn that simply adding shelves in your closet can increase space. It is easy to build shelves with the proper materials. Talk to your local hardware shop about the best ways to put shelves in closets and cabinets.

The furniture you choose for your bedroom makes an enormous difference to the appearance of your bedroom. When you buy the furniture, ensure you are keeping an efficiency goal in your mind. Consider furniture with dual functions. Consider mirrors that double as a storage space. Pick a chair that could be used as a bed should unexpected guests want to stay over.

If you are arranging your furniture, make sure to position them towards the corner of your room. For instance, angling your couch to the corner will enable you to leave an area behind that can be used to keep things like umbrellas or CDs.

Tips for a successful life Your Bathroom

Cleaning and maintaining a functional and clean bathroom is essential for the hygiene of your family. There is no need to spend a lot of money on bathroom items just for maintenance. Here are a few options you can take to help you improve the bathroom.

In bathroom space, make sure to maximize the space. It is possible to achieve this by being creative in the storage of your belongings. You can make use of a variety of household objects to create a more efficient storage.

It's possible to use a spice rack to the storage of your toiletries in bottles like shampoos and lotions. If you have a bathroom that is shared hang coat hooks to help with storage of towels that are not in use. To store extra towels to be stored, roll them up as you put them away since they will take up less space. This will make your bathroom appear like a the spa.

Make use of small storage solutions in order to make it easy to locate your belongings. Place large containers in the sink and refill them when needed. Utilize a magnet strip to arrange your hairpins or bobby pins clips to your mirror.

Pick a big mirror in your bathroom. It's a great idea since it allows you to view your complete self when you dress. Apart from that you'll also believe that your bathroom is larger since a mirror gives an illusion of height.

Life hacks to Your Lawn & Garden

Your front lawn is the first thing people see when they view your home. It is important to keep your lawn tidy to make the best impression to your guests and guests. Additionally grasses can be quite large. You'll be able to increase the size of your lawn when you are aware of tips and tricks to live by to assist you.

The most basic method to make your life easier is to transform an empty milk container watering container by piercing holes into the cap. If you want to create an instant shade during the summer months, you can employ a regular curtain to protect your plants. Install one end of the curtain on your house , and the other to the pole or tree and then slide it across when needed.

Cleaning garden tools is difficult. To remove dirt and dust from your garden tools, you can take pieces of aluminum foil crumpled and soak them in water. Utilize the aluminum to clean away any dirt or debris that you do not would like to see. If your tools appear old and rusty can apply white vinegar to to dissolve the corrosion.

Life hacks for your Garage

Do not make the error of not taking care of your garage. Garages are filled with dangers, which is why it is crucial to store your belongings in a way to keep your garage secure. Also, you must do all you can to ensure your garage is secured. It houses a variety of costly tools, and it could also be used as storage for your vehicle as well. It is imperative to ensure that you keep criminals from your garage to ensure the security of your family members as well as your home.

The most fundamental thing you can follow in order to maintain your garage tidy is to keep everything out of the garage. in it. Put away all everything that isn't essential.

Here are a few other tricks that can aid you in maximising space while at the same time ensure that your garage is safe from accidents.

Simple curtains can be a boon to make your garage appear more inviting. Whatever you do to put your tools in shelves or baskets but they won't look appealing to the eye. To add aesthetics put curtains up on the wall in front of the storage area. Just slide the curtains in, and you'll instantly be able use the second half of your garage in any way you like.

To keep your belongings in your garage, it's an ideal idea to construct an upright shelf that can put your sporting goods, tools and other things. They are fairly simple to construct. Find the necessary materials at the hardware store, and get started making your shelves today!

One thing to be aware of is how you place your car in the garage. Utilize pools of noodles for cushioning your walls from bumps that might happen in your vehicle. Cut and screw pools of noodles on the garage's walls to help cushion the impact to your car's doors. This will help you save hundreds of dollars on painting. If your vehicle has scratches, you can use nail polish to hide the scratch.

The garage of your home is full of valuable things that could draw burglars to your neighborhood. Be sure to secure your garage, as apart of containing costly tools and equipment such as your vehicle and other vehicles, it also serves as the main entrance to your house. Install the motion sensor light. one that senses motion is the best choice. The light should be placed so high that it is difficult to break or take apart.

Cleaning up the Space around the house

Do you feel that you're surrounded by many things? Are you annoyed that your home appears so small due to having too numerous possessions?

Few homeowners take note of the management of space. They think they must have larger homes in order to make more space. However, an effective space management system is needed for making the space more useful. Your home is able to hold more items when you know how to organize them correctly.

You could, for instance, utilize a tension rod within your sink cabinet to make an horizontal bar to hang your cleaning spray bottles. Imagine the floor space you'll conserve!

There are numerous other methods to use! Be creative with your surroundings. For instance, tissues boxes and cardboard tubes work great for storing plastic bags in a neat manner. Look around your home! What are the things you could change?

I hope that you've uncovered at the very least a few useful tricks and tips in the book thus far. If you've done an opportunity, I'd love it that you make a point of leaving an honest review about the work on Amazon and this is done via this link. Thank you!

CHAPTER 2: LIFE HACKS FOR YOUR OFFICE

At work it is crucial to create a pleasant and positive atmosphere. Don't let yourself get overloaded by clutter or small things that could be accomplished faster and with less effort. You'll be a much more productive worker if you're in a relaxed working environment. If you're better at your job, then you stand a greater chances of becoming successful in your professional career.

If you're spending long hours trying to tidy your office, you are increasing your productivity down. That is you're not making the most of your time at work in your role as an employee. If you know our office hacks and tricks, you'll be able to finish your work efficiently and quickly way. Additionally, you will be in a position to save money on office equipment! The general rule is that life hacks can help you become an employee who is more effective!

Are you wondering about the strategies you can apply to become more productive as an employee? Here are a few simple tips to assist you in becoming an efficient and productive employee.

Use nail polish to seal envelopes

The act of licking envelopes is unsanitary! You could even develop an irritated tongue when you frequently lick. The best way to prevent this is to apply a nail polish that is clear. It can seal the envelopes and is not removed through steam.

Make use of a can opener when opening office products

A can opener can aid in opening the plastic containers such as a jar filled with glue. Don't be stressed about an issue that is easily solved with a simple fix.

Protect your passwords

It is essential to protect your passwords for keeping your online accounts safe. Do not use dates and names as they are easily identified. Do not use personal information for your password too. Make sure to use phrases or words from a foreign language that you know. You could also choose patterns that are easy to remember. It is recommended for you to alter your password every few months.

Fitness and fitness

A chair that is sat on all day long can do harm to your body over time. You can exercise by switching your chair to an exercise ball with a big size. Do some movement every now and then. Move your body so that it gets some movement. If you have an adjustable desk, that's the perfect solution.

Toilet paper rolls to arrange cords

When you use toilet paper rolls, you'll be amazed at how simple it is to keep your cords free of knots. You just need to place the cords vertically into the rolls of toilet paper. If you'd like to, wrap the rolls or color them however you like to make them look more attractive.

Notes with sticky notes to keep your keyboard

If your keyboard is full of crumbs and dust, you'll have a hard working. One easy way to get your keyboard clean is to utilize the sticky side of a note. Place it into those spaces in between the keys, and dirt will adhere to it.

Egg Carton to prevent your laptop from overheating

Overheating is a typical issue for laptop users. You can avoid this issue using a placer in an old egg carton. It will keep the laptop from becoming overheated.

Adhesive wall hooks for mounting your tablet

Use hooks made of plastic to place your tablet on the wall like TVs. Get a few, and take care to position them so that your tablet can comfortably be seated on them when you wish to watch something.

Ruler and Smartphone - Smartphone ruler

It's recommended to capture a photograph of an ruler. Make adjustments to ensure it is correctly aligned. This can be used when you suddenly need to gauge something.

For presentations

For any visual presentation the white text with a black outline is more easy to read. Make sure your font's size select is the right size. Beware of confusing fonts and stick to what is professional looking. Don't overburden your presentation with phrases. Use keywords that make your point clear.

Make Peace

Secretary, technical support and janitors are truly the powerhouses in the office. Meet new people; keep track of birthdays and have everything you need!

CHAPTER 3: REDUCING STRESSS AND INCREASING PRODUCTIVITY

Our lives are a constant source of stress

We've all been taught to put in the hours. Although this is a great way to get the task done, it usually results in emotional stress. If you're always stressed due to your job, your health is likely to be affected.

It is impossible to completely eliminate stress. Stress is an integral aspect of working in a professional setting. Every professional is aware that it is an essential element of work.

You can discover how to manage stress. Manage stress in a way that is healthy to ensure that it doesn't harm your body. Stress shouldn't be a factor in your life. Don't let stress rule your life. What can you do to be able to enjoy life If you're always worrying and stressed?

If you're always feeling stressed, it's the perfect time to alter your routine!

Here are some suggestions that will help you deal with stress.

Top Tips For Reducing Stress

Stress management is primarily about maintaining your health. Whatever your situation is due to your job, make sure you provide yourself with the care and attention that you require to ensure your body is healthy. Make sure you take at least five deep breaths before you begin your day, to help you prepare for the rest of the day. Move around while on the mobile to receive the proper quantity of physical exercise. Be careful not to eat too much when you're traveling or working.

Breathing can be a great way to relieve stress and gain positive energy. It is a technique that is used in meditation and yoga. If you are stressed Take deep breaths to release any negative energies.

Remember that the food you consume impacts your mood. Be careful not to fill your body with too many calories that it will cause you to feel slow and slow.

It is essential to organize your budget in order to stay clear of overspending. You should reserve a part of your income for savings. Get a small binder and divide your funds according to the needs that need for payment. It is also recommended to put your money into mutual funds rather than saving it in banks.

Set small daily goals to help you get what you'd like to achieve. When you start your week, you should have a decent idea of the goals you'd like to accomplish. Your schedule is flexible enough to allow you to adjust it however, you should at the very least , you should have an idea of what it is you'd like to prioritize. You should create a checklist to ensure you don't forget any important thing.

It's always a great suggestion to have positive people who help bring out the best of you. Negative and toxic people can make you feel down. They make you feel dismotivated and you're likely to be discontent if you have negative people constantly around you.

Each time you experience something that you believe could increase your chances of obtaining an interview, you should make sure to update your resume as quickly as you can. It's important to update your resume. It is impossible to predict what day your dream job could be knocking at your door. Maintaining your resume prepared to go can give you hope and help you be prepared for any opportunities may come your way.

Productivity

Many people believe that as long as you're doing your best, you're productive. It's not true at all. The most efficient people have plenty of free time. This is due to the fact that it is essential to think intelligently rather than work for hours.

The truth is even when you're working it doesn't automatically mean that you're achieving. You must ensure that you're doing your best work if you really desire to be successful.

What can you do to increase your efficiency? You will only be efficient if you're able to concentrate your attention, time, and enthusiasm. Here are some tips to help you become more efficient at work.

Do not multitask.

When you are multitasking, you give an illusion of doing many things, you're in reality not. Your attention is constantly moving from one task to the next. Each when you switch your focus the brain needs some time to adapt. If your mind is focused on some goal, you're better able to accomplish more in a shorter period of time.

Instead of trying to do several things at the same time instead, concentrate on completing the task in one area before moving onto the next. It's not as difficult as you imagine!

If you are looking to concentrate then it is recommended to work in a space in which you can be productive. Be sure to have your work space stocked packed with all the items that you require to eliminate any distractions.

There are times when everything is not urgent.

If you get e-mails at the end in the morning, do not think that you must respond immediately. It's true that you don't have to do so, unless it's an issue of life or death.

It isn't necessary to go through everything you get. It is important to learn how to filter information and avoid distractions. Also, you must learn to prioritize. Make an sketch of how you'd like your day to unfold and do not let the tiniest of e-mails keep you from your goals.

Begin with a little bit of time

If you're a company employee, then you have no choice but to stick to the company's schedule. It's best to begin arriving 15 minutes prior to the actual hours of work to stimulate your mind. It doesn't matter what you are doing at work. The most important thing is to allow yourself enough time to adjust to work before you actually begin.

Exercise

It will help you stay energized and focused even when you're exhausted and weak. If you are feeling tired and tired, take a quick walk. A short walk can let your mind relax and help you become more productive.

Stop working

If you are spending too long doing something, your productivity will suffer as well. It's not just about the amount of time you were working. It's equally about how productive you're.

Make sure you have enough time to relax. Human beings aren't perfect, and you only have the capacity to achieve the maximum amount. Don't be too ambitious and over-work yourself.

Start habits

Start with a small amount, then gradually preparing yourself to accept larger goals. If you begin with a huge goal right away and fail to achieve it, you'll likely get dissatisfied. Most of the time people who establish positive habits later develop discipline and become productive. It's not easy to start and the little modifications they make can help them to improve their lives dramatically.

CHAPTER 4: TRAVEL HACKS

Travel can be an enjoyable trip. But if you don't prepare the right way, it can be tiring and stress-inducing. It's more enjoyable if you prepare the right things which will make your trip more enjoyable and smoother. You'll definitely gain from having planned and put everything in order before you take off on your plane.

There are a myriad of possible things that can be wrong while traveling. Even experienced travelers do make mistakes. Why make the same mistakes when you could avoid and avoid them with just some simple steps?

Travel hackers are those who are who are always looking for the miles and rewards or elite status. Do you believe you're a successful travel hacker? Here are some helpful tips to assist you.

Travel Tips to Pack Your Things

The process of packing things can be an effort. In case you do not pack things properly, you could be left with a bunch of luggage or even overlook something important to your travels. Here are some tips that can make packing more comfortable for you.

Create a list. Be sure to take all the things you will need. If you're taking any type of medication, it is important to bring enough medications to last the duration of your travels. You don't want to be searching for pharmacies, particularly in a foreign location. It's difficult to describe what you require and the dosages for their tablets may differ. Additionally, you should consider packing essential medicines to treat fever, headaches and colds.

When packing your clothes, you must to make the most of space so that you don't need a large suitcase. If you don't want to fold your clothing, you can try rolling them. This method has been proven highly efficient in saving space. Take a few classic pieces and mix and match once you arrive at your destination. If you're heading to a tropical island on holiday, it's an excellent idea to pack an elegant dress or simple casual outfit in case anything happens.

One great idea is to take a photograph of each suitcase when it's opened so that you can see what's inside each suitcase. So when you get there, you won't have to look to find which one has diapers. This is a great idea to travel with children!

If you're planning only a short journey then you can use straws to store liquids and creams. Be sure to secure them properly and place them in an airtight container to avoid getting a mess inside your bag.

Travel Tips Before You leave for a trip

Hotels can be expensive. If you're searching for a more affordable option look into houses available for rental (if you're traveling with your family) as well as a hotel room to rental (if you're traveling on your own).

Have you ever taken a long journey only to come back and you don't know where you parked your vehicle? Snap a quick picture using your phone BEFORE you leave the parking garage to remember which parking spot and level you took advantage of.

Check your visa and passport and ticket, then send the documents to yourself. It is also a good idea to remember your passport number as well as details of your flight if you can. This simple step will save you from anxiety in the event that you forget these crucial documents needed for traveling.

If you're going to the country of a foreigner, search for apps that will aid you in communicating with locals. It is not necessary to learn the entirety of the language. Select the right apps, and you won't have difficulties communicating with locals about your most basic needs.

If you're planning to carry your camera, don't forget to snap a photo that you are in first. This will show that the camera belongs to you in the event that you lose it.

Travel Hacks during your trip

Train passes are generally less expensive if you reserve them in advance. If you wish to book your entire trip in advance. Imagine how much money you'll save by planning your travel itinerary in advance. All you need do is check the websites of the train companies operating in the country that you are visiting.

Make the most of breakfast buffets. Get your stomach full to ensure you don't have to have to spend a lot on food. Some restaurants allow visitors to bring food items before they leave. Make use of their kindness. Most often locals are willing to assist tourists in enjoying their journey.

Make sure to remember the address the place you're staying. It is advisable to carry an address card from the hotel to keep in case you become lost. It is always possible to give that card and it will make it easier to locate the way back to your home.

While certain countries may offer discounts or tax credits for tourists There are also sellers and sellers who profit from tourists who aren't informed about the proper price. Do your research and don't appear as if you're going to be able to trust everything you hear. If you are a tourist, you must be aware to avoid scams as well as other kinds of problems. However, when you travel in Europe make sure you look for the VAT FREE logo at a store. Depending on the country you're in and what you are buying, you can get 19% discount off your cost of the purchase!

When you visit tourist areas One of the most effective methods for saving money is to take bottles of water. It is inevitable to be thirsty frequently if you're immersed in walking. Make sure to refill your water bottle every time you can.

It's a good option to make use of the internet to ensure your security. You should ensure that you are searching for scams you might be susceptible to. Do your research. Blogs are great because they provide information about your experiences. You should read the blog before you leave. It's never too early to know when some unexpected information could prove useful. One tip is to download the app CityMaps2Go, which is free to download a Google-based citymap of all major cities. It doesn't require any data plan to use the app, and it acts as a GPS as well! In addition, you'll find Wikipedia articles available within the app so you can plan your own walking tour around the city. Here's the link to test the app.

Traveling can be stressful if you're not prepared. If you are able to efficiently plan everything out you can reduce the stress.

Don't forget to enjoy yourself while you travel! Create friendships and lots of memories.

CHAPTER 5: MEMORY HACKS

Have you ever found yourself in a situation where you don't know who you're speaking to? Are you having trouble remembering a telephone number? You may be a college student always having trouble remembering what you've learned? In the present day we receive lots of information. We are constantly trying to keep track of every detail.

When we were young, we had very sharp memories. But as time passes and we age, the majority of us have difficulty remembering things in a timely manner. It's like having a muscle and it must be exercised and conditioned for a while if you wish it to be more effective and efficient.

Ideally, writing down information and then repeating them over and over repeatedly is the best method of retaining particulars. But, we don't have this convenience all the times. There are instances where you need to keep your mind on the go. There is no need for extraordinary powers to keep track of passwords and client names. There are a variety of techniques and tools that will aid you in remembering the things you require.

Don't underestimate the power of your brain! If you put in the proper amount of repetition you'll be able improve your memory within a matter of minutes!

Here are some hacks for memory that you may consider useful.

Nap and rest

How can you remember things in the event that your brain is not fully charged? Sleeping enough and getting enough rest assures that your brain will be capable of processing new information. Apart from the usual eight hours of rest at the night, take a nap during the day. A short nap of 15 minutes will do wonders for your brain and consequently, your memory too.

While working your brain is essential but you should take time to let it relax as well. Don't test your brain's limit constantly. Being on the go for a long period of time can surely harm the brain cells. Like any other muscle the brain requires regular rest and rest.

It's not about being smarter. In most cases it's about knowing how to utilize your brain in a way to be able to recall the information that you need to remember.

Here are some strategies that will help improve your memory and have better memory generally.

Learn to concentrate

In our modern-day world multi-tasking has become a common buzzword. Many people enjoy the challenge of trying to accomplish a lot simultaneously. However, this method of doing things can be quite problematic. When you're multitasking it is difficult to grasp the information. Additionally the fact that you aren't able to absorb all the information. This makes it hard to remember and recall.

Remember keywords

Keywords are extremely effective in helping people remember important details. If you are faced with a lengthy piece of material such as a historical essay make note of the keywords to aid in remembering what you need to remember.

Choose words that are powerful enough to help you remember many details about the topic. Avoid trying to recall a large number of words, since that defeats the goal of this strategy. The most important thing is to pick effective ones that let you gain a deeper understanding of the information you're trying to retain.

Use repetition techniques

If you can say something loud, it becomes more easy for the brain retain details. For instance, if you meet Gina introduce yourself to her by saying the phrase, "Nice meeting you, Gina." Try to repeat the name a few times during your conversation. Repeating the name repeatedly and again will help to re-incorporate it in your mind.

Make your own Mnemonics

Mnemonics, also known as patterns of words, letters and phrases are a great way to keep things in mind. When you use mnemonics you're actually making use of your senses to recall details. This makes it easier for your mind to absorb and remember information. Utilize your sense of humor to recall things with ease. Make positive images that assist you in remembering the crucial information you need to remember.

Train your brain

Develop your brain's ability to think more by doing exercises like board games and puzzles. The games of crossword, scrabble and Sudoku can be beneficial to your brain. Also, you can engage in memory games to keep your brain active. The more you exercise your brain and the better it performs, the more efficient it becomes. These simple games could help to prevent Alzheimer's or other brain-related diseases.

Engage your senses

The more you engage your senses in learning something new the more easy it will be to be able to recall crucial information later in the future. It is best if you know which kind of person you are. Some learn better by using their body. Some do it by visualizing pictures. Some learn by singing. Find out the way you learn This will make it considerably easier to recall the information you have learned.

For those who learn visually it is possible to transform text into pictures. For learners who prefer to hear you can choose the tune or song that can help aid in learning and make it more efficient. Determine which kind of learner you are so that you can optimize your learning experience.

Note it down

If you are able to note down your thoughts take the time to take note of it. The simple act of writing down the crucial details in your mind. You don't have to go back and read the notes you made. Simply using a pen to write random notes stimulates brain cells, making it easier to recall information that you may need later on.

Don't believe that it's identical to writing on a keyboard or a touch screen. It's the act of writing that makes it easier to remember, as it stimulates your body. Yes writing on the keyboard can be faster and more efficient. But, it does not stimulate your brain as deeply as writing does.

Exercise

You should know that exercising can bring many advantages. It's not only good for your body but can benefit the brain as well. Your memory will be sharper when you exercise. This is because exercising will help you let your mind be free of anxiety. With a clear head you'll be able to recall crucial details.

Chapter 6: 17 Online Hacks To Save Money And Make More

The first hacks we will be introducing will be focused on making use of the internet to earn and save money.

#1: Create multiple accounts on eBay to increase the price of items you Are Selling

When you sell your product on auction websites such as eBay the amount buyers will offer you for your product is contingent on the price that competitors are willing to pay. You can increase the price by creating artificial competition making the following changes:

Step 1.

Post the item that you would like to sell

Step 2.

Create several additional eBay accounts by using an VPN that lets you create accounts that appear like you're in a different state, or country.

Step 3.

Compete with other bidders for your product, causing real buyers to increase their bids to their full potential.

Step 4:

Utilize multiple accounts instead of just one when you outbid yourself to make it appear that the item is highly sought after to make buyers believe that spending a large amount of money for it is sensible.

Be sure to use an IP address that is correct for every eBay account and delete your cookies every attempt to switch your account.

#2 # 2: Netflix Movies to Watch Without A Account

If you're not looking to sign up for an Netflix account This is how you can enjoy movies without one:

Step 1.

Google the movie you'd like to watch, and then include "Google Docs" in quotes to obtain an exact match.

Step 2.

You will receive URLs to web sites where these movies are stored in their drive accounts.

Step 3.

Log in to download the films for free. In some cases you can even stream the film on the internet.

#3 3. Crack A Seller's Spirit on Craigslist

If you're looking to buy something from Craigslist it is possible to get it at a low cost by creating the impression of the vendor offering the item for sale for a high price. Here's how:

Step 1.

Make three or four fake emails.

Step 2.

Utilize fake email addresses for sending messages to sellers telling them that you're interested in the item , but say over the purchase price. too expensive.

Step 3.

Use your real account to offer lower than the seller's price but higher than the offer you'd made on the fake accounts previously. The seller may think they've taken advantage of you, even although it's the opposite about.

#4: Find successful GoFundMe Business Opportunities, and copy them

It's difficult to come up with the most innovative and creative ideas that will catch the attention of people. You can stay away from being creative through the following methods:

Step 1.

Explore the internet for new business concepts that have proved successful on GoFundMe campaigns.

Step 2.

Copy the idea , only modify a few minor things like the branding and claim that the idea was original to you.

Step 3.

You can raise capital to fund your business

#5: Subscribe to YouTube Premium for a Bargain

If companies offer online services to emerging markets and charge a much less expensive price than they would to regular Americans who live in the US.

YouTube Premium subscriptions cost $11.99 monthly in USA however it is just $3.15 to Russia. You could get a discount of $8.84 monthly by joining YouTube while making your account appear as if you're the Russian native, rather than an American.

All you have to do is to use an online virtual private network (VPN) to create your IP address appear as if it's from any country that you wish to around the world.

#6 Read online subscription News For Free

Have you ever wondered how subscription-based news sources can tell when you've hit your maximum amount of daily reads? It is due to the cached cookies data stored in your browser.

Go to the settings page to clear all history and cookies, then your web browser should be excellent as new. You can then read through the subscription platform at no cost as often throughout the day as you wish.

#7: Threaten To Cancel Your Cable Service

If you'd like to pay for half of your monthly subscription all you have to do is contact the company that you are using to inform them that you are discontinuing your service for the month of the issue. It can seem like you're trying to be friendly by calling them to provide an advance warning. Do you

If they ask you the reason for your departure when they ask why you're leaving, explain to them you've found a lower cost alternative to their services. They will attempt to convince you to stay by giving you a couple of months of less.

The trick to sell this is to convey that as if you're a polite person who isn't looking to leave the business without stating the reason.

#8: Earn Money from Hipster Preferences

Hipsters are drawn to handmade products, made by hand, over items made from "evil companies."

You can profit from these beliefs by purchasing products for sale at Dollar Tree, mark up the cost by a factor of five, and then sell the items on Etsy as handmade items.

It is also possible to add phrases such as organic and environment friendly to make them more popular with the hipster crowd. This is a win-win for all parties.

9: Get Netflix for Free

Netflix provides a free 30-day trial for all new subscribers. It is possible to take advantage of this opportunity to receive the services for free for the rest of your life. All you have be able to create is an email address that is fake on platforms that permit multiple accounts for email, such as proton mail. You can sign up with this email address and then make use of NETFLIX for a period of 29 days prior to making a decision to cancel your subscription. You can also create an email address that allows you to go through the process again.

Utilize an VPN to hide your IP address, so your platform is not able to identify you. Also, ensure you clear your browser of all cached data and cookies. Utilize VISA gift cards when filling out the section for payment.

#10: Claim Your Goods Never Arrived

If you are using platforms such as eBay which directly connect sellers and buyers it is easy to create an account, and then look for items of low value from sellers with high power. Purchase what you need and, when it is delivered you can contact the seller to inform them that the item did not arrive. The seller will give you a refund to keep you out of their way, particularly when you threat to leave a negative feedback.

Make sure that following every deceit, you set up an account with a fresh account so that you can duplicate the procedure in order to avoid having to be flagged for having too many issues on your account, and your IP address could be blocked. Also, ensure that you do not sign up for the delivery.

11: Steal Magazine Subscription Details

Many waiting rooms offer magazines to browse while waiting to be served. They often include online versions that have the same content.

If you happen to be in the waiting room of your dentist make a photo of your magazine's details address as well as the barcode that you printed. Sometimes this will give access to online versions at no cost.

This method works for a fraction of the time in situations where the need for a password isn't necessary. You could save lots of money and gain access to magazines that cost a lot of money in this manner.

#12: Clever Ways To Avoid Ads Online

The internet is one of the greatest inventions in human history but, as with every other invention there is a major negative side: the annoying ads that appear to be following you around.

They can be avoided by following these steps:

Step 1.

Find ways to block ads that are specifically targeted to specific software applications. For instance, you could make use of 'ad blocker' to block ads for Chrome as well as Firefox browsers. You can also purchase Brave browser , or YouTube Vanced to block irritating advertisements.

Step 2.

Learn how to add websites to your whitelist that require users to pay to gain access. The web designers have been catching on to this tactic and it is important to know ways to block websites which are blocking users from blocking advertisements.

#13"Destroy Your Competition"

If you're looking to purchase something from Craigslist and do not want to compete with other bidders, then you can get rid of the rivals by creating a similar listing and offering the exact item at a lower price. This will draw other potential buyers to make bids on the fake offer, while you actually make a bid for the item you're looking for.

When you've got what you need then you must take down the fake message you posted because you cannot deliver something that you don't really possess.

#14: Stay Away From Annoying YouTube Ads By Using This Trick

Make the URL change on youtube.com to YouTubeSkip at the top of the video that you are watching and you'll never see advertisements on the video. You'll save lots of time and save yourself many hours of boredom by just copying and pasting the word "skip" every time.

Note: Since YouTube depends on advertisements for revenue, and that's why YouTube is free This could be morally unsound.

#15: Play the "Good Samaritan" to get free Stuff

The most effective method to gain something from someone is to make it appear like you're not interested in it initially.

Step 1.

Make use of the product you purchased.

Step 2.

Contact the company and inform them you are a faithful customer who observed something amiss with one of their products. would like them to fix.

Step 3.

Do not request them to exchange the item since it could lead to an argument. Instead, tell them that you're satisfied with their service in the past and put it aside. The company will then ask to refund you or give an additional copy of the item to ensure that you remain as a loyal customer.

#16: Learn To Pirate

Kanye West got himself into quite a bit of trouble after his video showed him buying music software through a pirate website, instead of purchasing it. Despite his wealth, he was determined to purchase the music software free.

Pirated websites such as Kickass Torrents and 1337x give users access to films music, software, and more, such as premium eBooks at no cost.

Here's how you can take advantage of this:

Step 1.

Software for downloading piracy, such as "BitTorrent" or "TransmissionBT.'

Step 2.

Go to a torrent site and look to find your files.

Step 3.

Click this magnet.

Important to know the laws of your country on the use of piracy. To protect yourself you should use VPN.

#17: Make use of free trial Phases of Software. Then, Delete the Trials before they expire

Software companies, particularly those that deal with antivirus software are offering limited-time deals that offer free services for just a few weeks or even months. When the offer expires and you are required to purchase the services.

A lot of people have realized that by deleting software prior to expiry, and later downloading it again and then re-downloading it, you begin the process over. To avoid this, some companies have now left a message on your device that indicates you've downloaded their software previously and this makes the trick obsolete.

One way to circumvent this is to locate the source of the code and remove it. Conducting a search on the entire system to find any remnants left of the software deleted will allow you to find the place it's located.

Chapter 7: 23 Simple Hacks To Save Money When Visiting Stores, Theater Hotels,, Restaurants

The tricks we will be discussing in this chapter can aid you to save money while shopping, dining out as well as theaters and hotels:

#18: Receive A Free Charger

If you're traveling, it's easy to overlook carrying the charger for your mobile phone. It is a good idea to make use of any hotel's lost and discovered section to receive the charger for free. Here's how to do it:

Step 1.

Go into any hotel and affirm that you had a sleep there.

Step 2.

You claim that you left your charger in the hotel during your stay there

Step 3.

They'll give you an unclaimed and found box that is filled with various chargers. Test them until you can find one that works with the charging port of your device.

Step 4:

Make sure you act confident and believe in what you're saying.

#19: Enjoy Games For Free Using GameStop's Return Policy

Here's how you can play no-cost games using GameStop's policy on returns:

Step 1.

Purchase a game at GameStop.

Step 2.

You can play with it for no more than seven days.

Step 3.

Return the game and request an exchange or refund. GameStop's policy allows you to take the games back provided you return the game within 7 days.

Step 4:

After you've received your money back, locate an alternative GameStop store and follow the same.

The most important thing to pull it off is not go back to the same GameStop store too often. Find multiple stores and go through them, so that when you're returning to the store you first visited they've already forgotten about you.

#20: Claim to be Diabetic to get away by eating food in the Theater

Some theaters have high prices for food and refuse to permit customers to bring their own food. Here's how to defeat the system.

Step 1.

Keep snack items inside your purses.

Step 2.

Enter the theater with confidence.

Step 3.

If a theatre employee spots you, make it clear that you are a diabetic that needs to keep blood sugar levels in check; the person is likely to let you go. To make the story more appealing take a simple instrument to help sell the story. By displaying the device it indicates that you are taking your situation seriously.

#21: Take Advantages You Get With Stature

When filling out forms for an hotel room, you should choose to use the word doctor rather than Mr. or Mrs. Prefixes with this prefix are usually very demanding. Because they are worried about angering you and being dismissed by the manager The staff will give you a particular consideration.

Always be sure to remind people about this status by using phrases such as "actually you're Doctor Morgan!" The paradox is the higher up and opulent you appear the more likely you are to convince people to believe in the fable.

#22: Receive a Free First-Class Seat

Sometimes, airline employees are exhausted and do not want to see your boarding passes. You can profit from this. Here's how:

Step 1.

Wear a nice dress like those who belong in the top tier of society.

Step 2.

You must be the last one to get onto the plane.

Step 3.

If the attendant isn't asking for your boarding pass go into the first-class cabin, settle in and act as who is part of.

#23: Drink Expensive Liquor For Cheap

The irony in life is the more wealthy you are the more people offer you gifts. You can benefit from this by visiting the most luxurious casino and receiving complimentary drinks.

This can be accomplished by exchanging $1000 cash in exchange for tokens. You can sit at a table and place the tokens easily visible. Blackjack or roulette, however, you can only bet at least $100.

Waitresses who see that you're high rollers and will serve your drinks at no cost. After you've finished drinking, grab your $900 or more and swap the cash back into. You'll have bought many high-end drinks at less than $100.

#24: Make Sure That Nobody will block your view at The Cinema

There's nothing more frustrating then going to the movie only to find a tall person sitting in the front of you, which means that you'll have to fight through the film to be able to see the screen.

It is possible to solve this issue by accidentally spilling a beverage on the seat next to you. When they see the stain, they'll immediately move away from the seat and leave you with the ability to see clearly.

Note: The most important thing to consider when selling this is using an alcohol that leaves an obvious stain to the furniture. So, choose Coca-Cola not Sprite.

#25 Get Free Food by pretend that you are Wed in the near future

If you're eating in a restaurant that provides catering services, it is possible to inform the waiters that you'll be getting married shortly. They'll offer free food tastings and then help you select the catering company they will use in your event.

When you're done your meal, collect the restaurant's contact information to ensure they believe that you didn't waste their time.

#26: free meals at Chipotle With a Debit Card That Doesn't Have Enough funds

Chipotle believes in providing services as fast as is possible, since any delay on the line is a waste of money. If you purchase food using debit cards that fail to allow the transaction to be processed Chipotle will believe it's an issue with the technology and provide you with the food without verifying the funds.

One Chipotle manager stated: "chipotle will let you leave if your credit card does not authorize , because the speed of service and effectiveness are vital in the long run."

#27: Claim You're A Walmart Employee

Walmart employees can avail discounts of 10% when they check into a variety of hotel chains. All you have to do is inquire whether they provide the discount while making your reservation and you could get the discount. Hotel employees rarely need to verify that you are actually an employee.

If you're looking to market the lie, you could walk around wearing an Walmart employee T-Shirt. Then, should they request an official badge for employees, tell them that you did not carry it.

#28: Movie Hopping Using One Ticket To Watch Multiple Films

This trick requires you to locate an open-air theater in an occasion when you are able to afford to spend a long time in the theater. This is how you purchase the tickets for a movie that is scheduled for earlier hours that day.

After the first film has finished take a trip to the bathroom so that security guards don't observe you. Wait until the second film is about to start and then stroll swiftly (but don't rush) into the second film that is playing.

The most important thing to make the work successful is confidence. If you behave as if you are a part of the group to a group, they will believe that you belong.

#29: Meals Free for The newly Engaged Couple

Find out about luxury hotels that provide free meals for couples who become engaged at their facilities. Dress in a nice way as if it's an important event and request your wife to remove her wedding ring. If you notice a tan line on her ring, discover ways to eliminate the line.

After dinner After the meal, sit down on your knees and invite her to marry you. Be sure to ask her in a stunning and emotional way. The bigger the show the better for you to promote the trick. The meal will be served for free, or at minimum, the dessert is free.

#30: Make A Friend That Looks Like You Buy Your Drink at Starbucks

If you happen to have a friend who is the same dimensions, eye color and weight, they will be able to help you purchase an costly Starbucks drink at no cost. You just need to walk in and make a purchase that comes with waiting time, and let your friend take home the beverage as if it was their own.

After your friend is gone you can go back and ask for your drink as if nothing had occurred. You'll get a complimentary drink so they can clear you of the way.

Restaurant chains simply cannot afford to keep customers waiting up the queue.

#31: Buy A Pricey Dress to Attend A Party, and Refund It The Next Day

It is only possible to pull off this technique one time per store, without attracting suspicion on you. Simply walk into a shop as if you're a regular customer and purchase your dream dress just prior to an important job interview or celebration. You can purchase the dress, go to any occasion you're required to go to, and then take it back the next day.

For you to be able to get away with this, you must first come up with an explanation for the reason you're returning the item. Some good reasons might be due to an allergy to the fabric or the size isn't what you want. Also, when you return the item, you dress appropriately to ensure you don't appear like someone trying to cheat the system due to "money issues."

#32 Take a look at weighing all your Organic Foods as regular food at The Self-Checkout Station

The benefits of organic food are that it is more healthy, however it is very expensive in comparison to regular food items. Self-checkout machines are unable to tell what is organic food and normal food items. It is possible to measure organic apples and oranges as regular and save cash on your grocery shopping.

It is possible to take it one step further and weigh expensive fruits less expensive once, however this is more risky because the sticker that reads "apples" but your bag clearly displays the sharp protrusions of the bananas will attract attention to you.

#33: Receive A Coupon for a Free Gift Card From Tesco

A friend should walk in front of you and throw a slippery wrapping down the ground. After they leave the location, stroll over and easily move the wrapper. The more impressive your display and the more impressive it is, the better for you. Tesco management will provide you with the chance to win a voucher for free to ensure you are happy.

The idea of suing them is not something they'd like to do since it could cause substantial financial obligations. It's not the best option for you as it could result in an extensive investigation of your background as well as a review of video footage of how the wrapper ended into the ground in the first in the first place.

You can use the voucher instead and you will receive lots of free things.

#34: Get a Free Meal In Exchange For A Made-Up Complaint

Have you ever wanted to dine in a high-end establishment but are afraid to blow your entire month's earnings for a single dinner? It is possible to play the system by dressing elegantly to appear like you belong to the elite crowd. You can then order the most expensive dinner you can find and consume three quarters of it.

Then, you can drop your hair long into the food, then abruptly take a break and show complete displeasure. Contact a server to voice your complaint and keep in mind that the more loudly you voice your complaints, the greater chances they will try to end the issue out of the fear of embarrassing the restaurant's other customers.

#35: Replace old tires with new Ones

If your car's tires are getting worn out or you're not able to afford enough money to purchase new tires, you could cut costs by obtaining free tires. The trick is simple:

Visit a car rental service and lease the latest, but identical model like your own. Take it home, and then swap the tires with the older ones. Return it to the rental business and pretend as if nothing took place. It is not often that they check they have identical particularly in the case of rental companies that are large and has hundreds of vehicles.

#36: Get Free Donuts

Dunkin' Donuts(r) is famous for their fresh, never-stale donuts. They do it by throwing out any leftover donuts after closing. If you'd like to receive many donuts for no cost, then take the final 10 minutes of the closing period in order to ask for them to hand you the donuts right before they dispose of them.

The employees are forced to choose other than to hand them over to you since the Dunkin Donuts management team states that employees are not allowed to carry any of the remaining donuts to stay clear of them. Therefore, they have to dispose of them or dispose of them.

#37: Access A Nice Bathroom

One of the most common problems in city life is finding a good bathroom particularly when you require it. In order to access an excellent bathroom visit a posh restaurant, sit down at an area, and pretend to read the menu for a few minutes. It is possible to request an ice-cold glass to help sell the scam. After a while, stand up and walk into the bathroom to take care of your business.

Then, you can relax then call your waiter and create a scenario such as the meat you eat isn't cruelty free or that you only eat at organic restaurants. This will enable you to leave the restaurant while looking outraged.

#38: Enjoy Free Meals at restaurants by pretending it's Your Birthday

A lot of restaurants will give you a freebie or something similar to your birthday. It's a matter of finding local hotels that provide this kind of service. They also have websites on the internet which allow you to sign up to your mailing list. You can choose different dates based upon when you'll be visiting each of the hotels, and then visit them at the exact dates you filled in.

Every time you visit make sure to mention your birthday in front of the workers. The tone you use should be casual and as easy as it can be. For instance, you could use the phrase "I am tempted to pamper myself with some delicious food today, since this is my birthday."

#39: Purchase A Car On The Cheap

Find an auction for cars that is sufficient to ensure that no one will see you among the thousands of cars. You can either go prior to the auction's official date or at the very beginning of the morning and look for the car you'd like to purchase. Remove a wire which will stop the car from running. You can then bid on the car while the other users avoid it like the way they would.

If the auctioneers manage to solve the issue but it's still going to appear bad for them since no one wants to purchase an automobile that has already had problems. It is possible to make a bid that is very low on something that other people believe is a bad idea. After you have won the auction, you can fix your issue and then take the vehicle to your home.

#40: Use the Coupon Code Military

A lot of businesses provide discounts of 10% or more for those who have served in the military forces. You can avail this offer when you shop on the internet. Enter the word "military" into the coupon field and you may be lucky. The majority of websites do not require evidence of military service.

Chapter 8: 7 Hacks To Help You Get The Best Out Of Your College Environment

These hacks can help you make the most of your college experience

#41 Reserving A Computer To Youself In The Lab

The computer labs in colleges can be crowded, especially when the time is near to exam time. Here's how to ensure that you have a space of your own.

Step 1.

Select a machine you would like to reserve. It should be one in the back of the lab, where there are the smallest number of eyes watching you.

Step 2.

Make an out-of-order notice and print it.

Step 3.

Shut down the computer then place the sign the front of it, and then you can use it as you please and be sure to put the sign at the end of each session.

#42: Utilize Augmented Reality to cheat on Exams

Augmented reality lets you utilize transparent materials like glass for creating images that do not interfere with normal sight. The medical students of Thailand have used this technique to cheat on their tests.

Here's how to make use of it:

Step 1.

Wear glasses that have enhanced reality capabilities, as well as cameras.

Step 2.

The glasses can be connected to the smartwatch.

Step 3.

The camera on the glasses will record images of exam questions and then transfer them to someone not in the exam room who will be able to find the answer for you.

Step 4:

The person then relays the information to you, and the results will display on your glasses or the screen.

#43: Make copies of student copyrighted Books

Students often have no choice but to buy excessively-expensive books to gain access to information that they will need for the semester. It is possible to download an online PDF version, print the pages and join all of the pages in one book. A textbook that is priced at $100 will cost you only $4.

Then you can offer the books at 14dollars, and keep the profits of $10 and save the students $86, which is the perfect win-win scenario for all affected. If you consider the situation, you'll see that this is an unpunished crime.

#44: Don't Take Responsibility for this embarrassing incident.

Imagine going to a college buddy's home for a celebration. When you go to toilet, you find the toilet in a puddle. Instead of letting others realize that you're the one to blame then contact the host and inquire what the location of you can find the toilet. After a while you can return to the host and say that the area is messy.

The logic here would be that the individual who reports the issue isn't the person who caused the issue. This is similar to the way that a murderer on the cop show would call the police on a crime scene that they created.

#45: Destroy A File before submitting it to Your Professor

If you're not finished with your homework but have to present it to your teacher You can submit the file in a corrupted state to save your time.

Step 1.

Select a file that has an identical extension to the one your professor requires you to send.

Step 2.

Visit corrupt-a-file.net and upload the file.

Step 3.

Send the file along with the name for the task.

#46: Do Not Submit The Correct Paper In Order To Receive A Revision To An Assignment For Class

To have extra time to complete the assignment you are assigned or homework, you may submit an essay in another class.

If the instructor notices that the assignment is not in connection with the class, you will be informed of your error and asked to turn in the correct assignment. This will allow you to get the time you'll need.

#47: Take People's Ideas and patent them before they Do

A lot of college students have brilliant ideas, but they don't have the money to either implement the ideas or even patent their products. Many don't realize the need to secure your ideas in a legal manner. Furthermore the process of patenting an innovative technological invention takes a lot of time and money.

You can profit from this by visiting college tech departments for ideas that you can get patents on. By doing this, you prevent other people from using the ideas you have created without paying royalty first. It isn't important who was the person who came up with the concept.

Chapter 9: 10 Techniques To Get A Job And Manipulate The Work Environment To Your Advantage

These tips can assist you in getting an interview and change the workplace environment to your advantage.

#48: Make Your CV to the At The Top Of the Pile

When you apply for a position in which a lot of other applicants are equally applying, you have to figure out how to be noticed by:

Step 1.

Find all the requirements listed on the website for qualifications requirements.

Step 2.

Copy them onto the CV with white ink. It is obvious to humans However, a scanner is able to read it.

Step 3.

If they must sort through the endless number of applications for jobs employers will make use of scanners on computers and keywords to identify CVs that meet their required qualifications.

When the scanner scans the CV it'll recognize your CV as having best qualifications and then send it to a person to be reviewed. Even if you do not have the qualifications required Your CV will now stand over all others.

#49: Submit multiple CVs in order to reduce the expectations of your potential employer

The best way to land an interview on the first attempt can be by proving to the prospective hiring manager so that when you finally arrive, you seem as a blessing them.

Here's how to do the following:

Step 1.

Make your CV and other CVs with various names as well as contact info. You should then submit them, preferring from multiple places, to ensure that your IP is unique.

Step 2.

If the prospective employer attempts to contact the other fake identities, but no one is willing to appear or even pick up their phone. company is likely to be dissatisfied.

Step 3.

If you get the call and you pick up the phone, make sure you are courteous and arrive for a physical interview at the right time. The difference between display of fake CVs and your manner of conduct will make you appear like the ideal candidate.

#50: Play A Convincing Sick Day

The secret to getting sick days is to convince people that you're sick. Here's how to accomplish it.

Step 1.

Relax on your back an inflatable mattress.

Step 2.

Do a dangling motion onto the edge to ensure that blood flows to your head.

Step 3.

Keep that position for three minutes, then contact your boss and inform them that you're not allowed to enter the office. Your voice will be a bit strange and convince anyone you are dying.

#51: Don't be a struggle when writing A CV

Making a resume can be a challenge particularly if this is the first time you've done it. To overcome this challenge, try joining a job search site and upload a copy of the kind of job you're trying to find. Many CVs will be coming to you. Then, you can select the one that you think you'll like the most and alter the name and gender. You can also combine the characteristics you appreciate from several CVs to make the perfect blend.

#52: Request A Reference from a Friends

If you're young and looking for the first position, many employers will not take you seriously because they don't have previous job experience. The ability to get a reference could be the difference between success and failure when it comes to getting that first gig.

The most effective way to overcome this issue is to have a person compose a great review of you. To ensure that the reference is credible you must ensure that the person is waiting for the phone call of the potential employer to confirm your good standing.

#53: Make Use Of A Special 2 For 1 Offer

If a restaurant is offering a 2-for-1 for 1 discount, and you're the only one at work conscious of the offer, you may make use of it to receive a number of free meals, or better yet, you can earn cash.

Tell everyone you're willing to feed everyone a lunch that day. Then, they must provide you with the money needed to purchase the meals. You could spend half the amount and give all of the meals to them, and keep the rest.

#54: How To Leave A Meeting without committing an offense

There's been meetings that were either boring or took too long with unneeded speeches. What can you do to avoid these situations, without being a target for criticism?

The best method is to create an alarm that will go off within five or ten minutes. After that, put the phone back in your pocket. The alarm could trigger the appearance of a phone call or message.

When it is time to beep you must get up and leave with your phone in your hand. Everyone automatically assumes that you've got an important or devastating information, and they do not bother to inquire about the reason behind the issue.

#55: Use Yourself as A Refutation

If you're skilled at impersonating voices and faking voices, this could be a great way to create a solid reference.

All you have to do is purchase unregistered burner phonesand make use of them as phone number of a former firm where you were supposedly employed. Keep the phone handy always to get the call whenever it is received.

#56: What to Do If You're Stopped Sleeping On The Job

If your boss notices you sleeping at work and it appears that you're about to receive an admonition, you can avoid this issue by saying, "The blood bank told me that this could occur."

You can do this in a loud voice to ensure that others who are around you can hear your voice. This will place you in difficult position , where criticizing the person who saved lives will appear unprofessional. You might even be given the rest of the day free.

#57: Keep A Photograph of Your Grandparents

When you apply for an opening, employers can inquire about any gaps in your employment background. One way to justify the reason you've not been employed for a long time is to state that you cared for the sick grandparents.

You should make it appear as if you took a break from your job to look at them when they weren't feeling well. You're likely to get an interview and the opportunity to be embraced to be a lovely person. A picture of an old man will assist in selling the deceit.

Chapter 10: General Life Hacks To Get The Best Out Of Life

These basic life hacks will enable you to make the most of life's opportunities:

#58: Carry A Helium Balloon To Take With You When transporting Drugs

It can be difficult for police to establish that you possess drug use even if they don't possess the substance in the first place upon your arrest.

Step 1.

Inflate a balloon and keep it in your vehicle.

Step 2.

Be sure to test the balloon to ensure it is able to handle the weight of the drugs.

Step 3.

If the police stop you when you are stopped by the police, tie the drug to the balloon, then let it go.

Step 4:

If someone asks what the balloon signified tell them that it was a present to your niece and that it was released accidentally.

Even if they are aware that you've just released the drugs but there's no way to prove it until they take it down. It is therefore better to go with a pale blue hue that blends with clouds and the sky as you fly away and make it difficult to be shot down.

#59: How to Participate In A Event

There is no way to stop the staff at a celebration in the event that they dress as if they're part of the group. Here's how to make the most of this:

Step 1.

Find a chef's jacket which matches the ones worn by the catering company that will be serving the event.

Step 2.

Pass by security in the event and talk to your mobile. Most people don't want to interrupt someone who are on the phone which increases the chance of being allowed to go right into.

Step 3.

After you have entered you can go to the bathroom, and wash the chef's attire since you don't want anyone on the catering team to label you as a fake. Make sure you are confident when you enter.

Note: A badge bearing an untrue name could be the key element which helps to make the lie seem more convincing.

#60: Use Your Mobile To Retake Stamped Photos

When you take a photo with your phone, it captures the phone's time and date, then tags the image accordingly-- sometimes, it can capture even geolocation data.

For instance, if you need to show that the hotel room or Airbnb was broken at the time the time you arrived, then you can employ this method.

Step 1.

Change the date and time of your cell phone.

Step 2.

Check the photo and make sure it's got the tag of the date in the past.

Step 3.

You can restore your phone's time and date to match the exact time, and then take a photo to prove that there was a problem at the time you entered the room.

#61: Concede The Perfect Crime

Have you ever felt so mad that you considered ways to be able to escape murder? Here's a trick to make it easier.

Step 1.

Cover the body with plastic to cover all smell as is possible.

Step 2.

Find a place that is deserted and dig a large hole.

Step 3.

Bury the body, then fill in the hole only halfway. Place a dead animal inside the hole and then bury it along with all the remaining dirt.

When a sniffer dog walks to a location when it smells something police will dig only to discover bones of the animal and conclude that's the scent that the dog was sniffing and then leave the scene.

#62: The Best Method To Create A Signature

Sometimes , in your life it is necessary to create an identity for any number of reasons. Here's the most effective way to go about it:

Step 1.

Take a picture of the signature.

Step 2.

Make a duplicate of the signature that appears on the document you must sign, but lower the opacity to 25 percent.

Step 3.

Make sure to trace an actual pen over the signature to get the perfect match

This method is excellent since a photocopy that is clear and unmistakable is simple to distinguish as opposed to using a pen to sign.

#63: Make a Deal With Someone Harassing You By Texting

The best method to take on anyone who has been harassing you via texts is to ensure they're so overwhelmed with phone calls they won't take the time to call you.

The most efficient way to do this is to list your name and contact number on Craigslist and offer an item for free. It should sound as if you've just purchased an entirely new device and do not require the previous one. You'll receive an interminable number of calls asking about the free product which makes texting difficult. You could even create several posts.

#64: Crash A Wedding For Food

Owen Wilson's iconic film from 2005 Wedding Crashers is a perfect illustration of how to attend weddings and also get free gifts. The character of Owen Wilson says in the film, "it's like fishing with the power of dynamite."

All you have to do is peruse the wedding announcements in your local newspaper's section and be sure to know the names of the bride and groom. You can also check their social media profiles to make sure you have more details about who they are as well as their families and acquaintances. The more details you have the more easy for you to be able to fit into their world and to be able to blend in once you're there.

Weddings are the most delicious occasions for food since people are always out in order to wow their beloved ones. This trick is definitely worth it.

#65: Purchase Something For Youself This Christmas That Your Partner Would Hate

Sometimes, your spouse won't wish to purchase something because it's too costly or due to a perceived moral dilemma. Take advantage of the festive time and purchase the perfect present and wrap it in.

If your spouse is asked by your spouse what the gift is Say it's a present from your boss and it's risky to reject the present.

#66: Free Parking

Parking in cities can be a challenge and the costs are also obscene. One solution to this issue is to make use of restaurants with valet parking that is free.

You can drive straight to the restaurant and hand your valet keys. Go inside the restaurant and locate the seat where you can watch the valet. You should wait until he appears busy, then leave the restaurant and leave without him noticing.

Take yourself to where you originally desired to go after which you return to the hotel, but preferably without the valet being aware of you. Then leave the hotel as if you had been there all day.

#67: Receive A Free Gaming Disc

Video game discs may get damaged so badly that they cease to function. If you don't want spend money on replacing the discs, then you could work the problem solved with a little savvy.

Simply walk into an online game rental store and make sure that the disc's cover is identical to your. You can rent the disc out for a day , and then return it and replace the rental with the scratched disc.

This is a great strategy However, you should be cautious not to use this more than twice. The store could utilize rental records to locate the individual who keeps returning damaged discs.

#68: Free Parking at the Mechanic

If you are you are stuck on the streets and don't want pay for parking, avail garage parking services that are completely free.

Car garages usually offer free services, such as wheel rotations and tire pressure tests. Tell them you'll return within a few hours to collect your car. Just like that, you'll get free parking while the mechanics work.

#69: Sign-Up For The Gym as a Gay Couple To Receive A Discount

Couples typically receive 50% off gym memberships when they join together. If you don't have a spouse but you have a friend in search of an exercise membership, join together as an openly gay couple. There is no reason to be suspicious because people are worried about looking homophobic.

#70: Get Blue Contact Lenses

There is a reason that some people like blue eyes. If you're hoping to have luck in the dating scene, consider wear blue lenses. You'll find that your chances of success are increased exponentially.

Note: Make sure you adhere to them in a proper manner, because if someone discovers that you're faking blue eyes, you'll be in hot water.

#71: Try swearing on Automated Voice Systems to get a human Operator

Businesses use automated voice services to meet customer demands without the expense of employing an employee. But they also recognize that these systems may be slow at certain times. So, they may program them to recognize swear words as a sign that someone is extremely upset.

If you're not keen on to deal in automated system, just use the following swear words. The system will connect you with an operator who is human.

#72: Breathe the Speed Limit without consequences

The dealer number plate is distinctive in that they allow drivers to go over the speed limit, without the risk of legal penalties. The reason for this is that the dealership would like the prospective buyer to determine the speed of the car that is why they need a real-world instance. If you keep the dealership's number once you have purchased a car you are able to keep using it forever, while also reducing the likelihood of police catching you exceeding your speed limits.

#73: Find The Best Place In The House

The stadiums at sports have seats reserved for tickets with higher prices. These seats are rarely sold entirely, which is the reason you should take a look at them since their views are almost always superior.

To achieve this goal To achieve this, log on to Stubhub to find seats that are unlikely to be sold, and then on game day, be there like you are a part of the team. In most cases, when you act as if you're entitled it is assumed that you are.

#74: Find A Wedding Space for Cheap

In the process of acquiring an area to hold your wedding, it's not wise to inform the vendor you are planning to use that you're planning an event. In the event that you tell them, your cost will automatically increase. It can be referred to as an event or a reunion. You'll save money when you don't use the word "wedding."

#75: Eliminate Parking Fees By Acting Like You're Part Of A Construction Crew

Certain jobs, such as taxi and private investigation depend on parking in only a couple of spots for long durations. Paying for parking spots on a regular basis could be extremely expensive quickly.

However, it's possible to make people let you go by making it appear as if that you're a member of a construction team. The majority of people do not worry about construction workers because they think that they are employed by the city.

In order to pull off this trick To pull it off, you need to accomplish two things First, purchase four cones of plastic and put they on each of the corners of your vehicle. To sell the trick wear the safety gear used by construction workers to identify themselves.

#76: Take Advantage of Unmanned Entry Points for Tickets

A lot of ticket sellers at parking garages offer grace periods wherein when you are allowed to leave before the grace expiration date, you do not be charged any parking charges. If the entrance is completely automated and not manned and you are able to enter parking as usual, however, when the time comes to go out, you must walk to the entrance and purchase an additional ticket and apply it when you are leaving. This method only works for automated garage entrances since when there's a guard and they see you, they'll have a second ticket to enter.

#77: Ask Your Roommate To Help Clean The Room

If you live with someone else, but do not feel needing to clean, you could overcome this issue by finding a dating app that your roommate is using. Create their perfect partner by creating the ideal profile picture and personal style.

Make it appear like you are fascinated by your roommate and tell them that you would want to go to their place where they reside. Make sure to insist that you value a lot and that they should be clean.

On the day you are in doubt you'll notice that your roommate has the room appearing clean. You can then you can cancel the date in the end of the day, but keep your profile updated to be used the following time that you need to get the room clean.

#78: Enjoy A Peaceful Ride home

Some people are not introverts which is why, if you're in the taxi or Uber You might not want a driver that tends to be too interested in having a conversations.

To avoid this issue Make a note in which you state that you are deaf or muted. It will instantly cut off the conversation and allow you with a peaceful ride to wherever you're headed to.

Be sure to keep up your deceit throughout. It's embarrassing to ask a question while declaring that you are muted.

#79: Don't Want to Stay Up All Night

Certain people aren't able to fall asleep in the beds of others. If you're like that person, you could create an excuse for leaving by setting an alarm that has the identical tone to your call tone. You can set it to one hour after arriving at a home.

If the phone occurs, you could pretend that you're receiving a phone call from your landlord stating that your home is inundated or your boss telling you that there's a work emergency. This trick allows you to leave without making any enemies with your loved one.

#80: Get Free Talk Therapy

We live in a time in which we all could get some help every now and then. However, professional therapy can be expensive.

For free therapy, phone IKEA and ask for someone to help you build the most complex design you can find online. If you're a man then you can continue calling until you hear an answer from a woman.

During the duration of the call, you'll be able to steer your conversation off of furniture, and focus on other issues in the real world. It's an affordable method to receive some therapy for free.

#81 Save Peoples' Politically incorrect posts for Future Blackmail

We live in a society in which a few years old Facebook posts could derail the career prospects of someone.

You can build databases that contain thousands of politically incorrect comments. After a while, if they've already removed the posts, you can make contact with anonymously and demand that they be paid in Bitcoin or else risk being exposed.

This method can bring you thousands of dollars. All you have to do is be patient.

#82: Act Deaf To Avoid A Ticket

If a police officer pulls you over because of speeding, you may be able to get away with acting deaf. The challenge in communicating with them could be so difficult that the police is likely to let you go.

It is possible to have handicap signs hidden inside your vehicle specifically for such occasions. These little things can help to sell the lie.

Be aware that this strategy can be extremely risky if the cop is aware of how to communicate using sign language , but you do not.

#83: Keep Your License Plate from prying Eyes

The unique thing about skating board grip tape is the fact that it has the ability to hinder cameras from taking photos through blurring. Normal eyes can be clearly seen through it, however, cameras may be having a problem.

This little trick to prevent photographers from taking photos of your number plate , while still staying legal because the plates are visible.

#84: Get Services Quickly

When you try to reach for help the provider could keep you waiting for a period of time, if not for hours.

One solution to this issue is to contact the helpline and select to select the Spanish alternative rather than English. If the Spanish operator answers it, there's a high chance they'll also speak English too.

Inform them that you chose Spanish on accident, however, they'll likely be able to assist you regardless. Don't allow them the chance to deny you help; express your request right away.

#85: Get Free Cash from a Change Vending Machine

Insert something into the slot to change it Make sure it doesn't get taken out. Many people deposit 50 or 100 dollar bills in order to collect change only to see the change be stuck.

After a few minutes you can return and clear the obstruction and collect the cash that's built up. It is possible to earn more than an amount of money in a single day by doing this.

Be aware that you shouldn't repeat this at the same time or it may make you look like a nuisance or cause people to abandon the machine as it's failed frequently.

#86: Master the Art of Using The Mask to Your Advantage

Before the coronavirus pandemic when the coronavirus pandemic was sweeping through, if you were wearing mask while sitting on the bus, passengers were likely to stay clear of them, and you could not share seats with others or engaging in unneeded conversation.

However, the reverse is not the case, and if you aren't wearing a face mask it is assumed that you might try to transmit the infection, or at the very minimum, that it doesn't matter whether you are.

When wearing a mask ceases being required the wearing of a mask could be considered a nuisance This means that this method is effective mid-way through the pandemic as well as after the pandemic and.

#87: Don't Be Afraid Of The Second Screening at The Airport

At the airport The first thing you'd want to do to do is be marked for SSSS which is the second screening. This process can be time-consuming and intrusive, making it imperative to find methods to circumvent this issue.

To avoid this hassle to avoid this hassle, you can utilize the boarding pass from your smartphone to go to security, instead of using the physical ticket that is designated for secondary screening. TSA will not bother to verify any information; they'll let you through without additional screening.

#88: Don't hold someone's Baby

When someone has had an infant They often ask their family and friends to be able to hold them in a gesture of acceptance. Babies are adorable and can bring joy to the world However, there's always the risk of falling or injuring a newborn.

To avoid holding the baby of a stranger without causing offence Tell your parents that you're sick of an illness or have not been vaccinated and do not wish to put the baby in danger. Parents will appreciate you for being so careful and turning a potentially difficult circumstance into an opportunity for you.

#89 How To Get away houseguests

If your family members come to visit more often than they should Here's a quick and easy solution to discourage them from this. Change your existing furniture with a new set of uncomfortable chairs that leave guests in a state of discomfort when they sit down.

The guest you don't want will develop an unconsciously induced relationship of pain when they visit you. You will be rid of them without declaring to them that they're not wanted.

#90 The Best Way To Use A Nicotine Patch To Keep Your Good Half

If you are concerned that your partner or husband is planning to go away the next morning due to the fight, you can apply a nicotine patch to the night before they go to bed and then take off the patch before getting up.

If the person decides to break apart with you they'll confuse the withdrawal symptoms being free of the effects of the patch for a breakup. They will believe that they're physically dependent upon you.

Be careful not to get sleepy when using this method because should someone wake up prior to you and spots smoking a nicotine patch any issues you had will be ten times more severe.

#91: Trick To Look Taller Than You Are

If you're a small person, others may take advantage of your shortness to ridicule your appearance. Here's a trick to make yourself appear taller

Step 1.

Purchase a high-quality insole.

Step 2.

It should fit in your shoe , and then use it to look taller.

Step 3.

When you're wearing it, ensure that you wear an appropriate trouser or dress which covers your ankles; Otherwise, people might be able to tell that something doesn't seem right.

#92: Learn to Name People You've Just met by their names

If you ask someone you've met recently to their names, this can throw them off balance, and also allows you to control them.

In the beginning, they must consider whether you are friends with each other , and if they have forgotten your name. Since they are uncomfortable to ask what you're name is, they'll take whatever demands you put on them to rid you of them.

Note: The most important thing to achieving this is to have a calm and comfortable tone of voice when talking to them.

#93: Learn to Use Pseudonyms to conceal that You're Looking At Someone Else

Many who are found cheating are caught because they got a call from a number the name that is suspicious. It is possible to give your accessory a completely non-related name, like KFC Burgers. Names can refer to something that evokes something physical about them, e.g., red strings may be a reference to a person who has hair red.

#94: Teach Your Children to love you more

Put a piece of coal as a present to your child from Santa When they ask them why they got this, explain to them that it's because Santa believes they didn't obey their parents properly that year.

If they're unhappy, gift them an assortment of presents to present yourself as the hero and ensure that your child is in good behavior next year due to worry that Santa is going to punish them once more. You'll emerge looking as a mighty hero in the tale.

#95: Earn Cash from Your Aunt for Being Doing Nothing

Fortunately, or not the older generation isn't able to know how technology operates. Therefore, the majority of grandparents and aunties have to depend on younger people in times of need.

If your aunt is suffering from the performance of her computer, say that you can fix it, but just increase the mouse speed of the cursor by 50-100 percent. The computer will appear to be quicker, even though nothing has changed. The process of changing the speed of your mouse should take less than an hour.

#96 Get Your Spouse Freezed Out of All The Top Divorce Lawyers

If you feel the marriage you have is on the verge to fall apart and you are worried about your marriage's future, you can take care of the situation by visiting the best divorce lawyers in the local region. If you are in contact with them, even for just five minutes, could result in an ethical conflict of interests. This means that your spouse will not be able to find a qualified attorney for divorce, and will be forced to use 2nd and 3rd level lawyers, which gives you an advantage.

#97: Prevent Yourself from Changes to the Diaper of Your Baby

Here's how to prevent changing diapers for babies:

Step 1.

Begin to approach your child and sniff it. Then say"something like "Someone created an mess."

Step 2.

Take the baby to the next room , and pretend to change the diaper.

Step 3.

When your baby has caused a mess, remind your child's parent that it's time to clean it up.

Make sure to monitor your baby more often than you would normally because it's not good for a newborn to wear an unsanitary diaper for a long time.

#98: Blame the Kids For Your Error

If you happen to scratch the paint of someone's car while driving around you may be able to make you cover the entire paint job. It is possible to get yourself out of this mess by accusing the child who rides bikes in the vicinity. It's hard to hold children accountable for their actions because they don't understand.

#99: Investing In Unfair Mutual Funds

Many are concerned about whether their investment is going to certain areas of the economy currently classified as unethical, such as the production of animal meat and oil.

The lower levels of investment in these areas are resulting in lower supplies and higher yields. You can recognize these kinds of investment vehicles that are feared and invest your money into them.

#100: Emotional Manipulation During Negotiations Can Help You Find Better Deals

If you're in a discussion with an opponent It is beneficial to study your opponent first. The more you know on them, the simpler to utilize the information to your advantage.

For instance, you might learn that someone is strongly about a certain issue , like hunting of species that are endangered, such as white giraffes. It is then possible to make it clear in passing that your business contributes funds to a foundation that fights this cause.

CHAPTER 11: HOW TO BUILD YOUR ENERGY

1. When you wake up, ensure whether your first thoughts are positive ones. If you think it's an negative thought, then immediately change towards its positive side e.g. "I don't want to work' ...' (now include the word "positive") or 'but at the very least, I'm employed currently and I have cash coming in to the banks' (then an intention) and 'I'll begin to search for a new job that I'm interested in'.

There's a quote that I've read, and it has changed the way I think about the morning, as well as throughout my day. It's like this...

An Indian Grandfather informs his grandson, "I have two wolves fighting for my heart.

One wolf is vicious and envious, fearful and resentful.

"The other one is kind and compassionate, kind and truthful. He is serene, peaceful and tranquil."

The Grandson asks "Which Wolf will prevail?"

The Grandfather responds, "The one I feed".

Beginning your day with positive thoughts and keeping clear of negative thoughts can set you on the path to an optimistic day.

2. If you are waking up early in the day, the first time you get up take a drink of at least 250mls of drinking water (cup size) and 500ml, or greater is more beneficial (H2O with no added chemicals. Ionized water is my favorite). This helps to rehydrate your body and allow for clearer thinking while it rehydrates your brain.

Water is essential for each bodily function, and everything we do consumes water. According to the standard guidelines, the average person needs eight glasses of fluids daily plus more after exercising or living in humid or hot climate (sweating) or when we experience a headache, are annoyed, feel uneasy or have constipation. Making an effort to drink the first glass of water upon waking from a deep sleep has made a huge impact on my life.

3. Moving your body. Stretch out, up and back, bringing your arms up to the extent you are able, then, if you want to take a pose that resembles a cross-country skier. shift your arms forward and back to criss-cross the front. Then, run in place for a while (takes less than an hour). Take note that when moving, running or standing in any position, e.g. in the kitchen, waiting until food is ready to be cooked, or waiting for the bus to come or at any other time, ensure whether the knees of your feet are bent only a little bit. When bent over, push your feet in.

Consider your day's routines. Many of us are driving, walking a little and being at work for most of the time. Our Lymphatic System is based through the motions of our muscles and joints pumps. This is why movement is necessary to keep away unwanted and unwanted bugs. If, after an half an hour of unoccupiedness, particularly sitting going for a brief walk and stretching can be beneficial to your energy levels over time. Walking is more than just energy, it also strengthens our muscles too.

If you are working from your home, turn on an old-fashioned song and dance or practice a bit of Yoga e.g. It's the Warrior 1 & 2 and Downward Dog stretches. Another exercise that can be energizing is lying on your stomach flat on the floor, your elbows up by putting your fingers or fists placed under your their chins, bend your legs, and then cross the legs a few times (we often observe children doing this on their own and beg the question of why they have such enthusiasm!). These exercises will help awaken your brain, calm your mind , and trigger an increase in endorphins, an excellent feel-good body chemical.

4. Breathing. It is well-known that breathing correctly is an advantage to living and that clean, healthy oxygen is vital to our lives. The same is true for the Diaphragm muscles. What is the best

method of getting the oxygen or air to our lungs at the smallest difficulty? A lot of people suck air through their noses or through their mouths. This is fine as a alternative however, do this...Without using your mouth to suck the air into by expanding your diaphragm. Watch as the air naturally is able to flow through your nose or mouth.

If you've not tried this before, it might seem strange, as everything might at first. Therefore for a workout take a moment to open your mouth then exhale. Then, simply open and relax your diaphragm over a period of time (no taking a breath). Notice how effortless it is, and realize that you are not 'out or breath'. Also, you have not used many muscles in sucking in air through our mouths or nose. This requires energy. Take note that when you do this you'll feel much more calm and relaxed all over. In time, this way of breathing will become the normal. The air you breathe is the backup plan in extremely circumstances.

Note Take note of Asthma and allergy-related conditions that are not treated with normal medications in the bag - please refer to Section 7 "While In the Wilderness' No.12.

5. Get a nutritious breakfast. Based on the American Heart Association, of all food items eggs are the top source of energy-boosting protein. Edible berries e.g. blueberries, raspberries. Fresh fruit like apples are all loaded with the energy-producing nutrients. Peanuts and almonds are nutrient dense and high in magnesium and fibre , which are both proven energy boosters. However , do not serve peanuts or nuts in any way to other people without a prior warning since some individuals may experience an allergic reaction .

If you're running out of time to eat, then you can use a protein powder (milk soy, milk, etc.) shaken with some powdered greens and any other ingredients e.g. macca, cacao, tiny amount of turmeric (a trustworthy source says to add a tiny sliver from white pepper in order to help activate the tumeric) along with a little honey, a pinch of oil of your choice, etc. This can be made using a shaker that you hold fairly quickly. It will also tie the drink for a time.

6. Daylight - Exposed your skin and body to sunlight of the day even when the Sun isn't shining. 10 to 15 minutes of sunlight exposure aids to clear any Melatonin left (refer No.13 Sleep, below), and boost your Serotonin, our bodies natural happy feeling hormone/neurotransmitter . It also aids in maintaining the vitamin D essential to our bodies. Therefore get up as early as you can throughout the day, take your time and enjoy the day's sunshine.

7. Focus - Throughout the day it is easy to get overwhelmed by many things. This reduces our motivation and can lead to feel stressed. Mindfulness Training is an effective way to reduce the stress. Mindfulness Training can help us not be overwhelmed by the ever-present future thoughts and memories of our past. It can

easily be summarized as paying attention to what you are doing now.

8. Consume healthy, regular food items that contain Antioxidants in them . Antioxidants are produced naturally in our bodies in a certain amount but certain foods boost the amount of antioxidants to the required amount. They maintain our body's balance of free radicals in good order. Free Radicals eradicate our Blood Cells. They are also produced by our bodies, however in greater quantities than antioxidants! The benefits of eating food high in antioxidants are well acknowledged by our hearts eyes, eyes, skin memory, ageing as well as mood balance, the urinary tract, immune system and even our energy levels and much more. Our levels are boosted through eating plant-based food e.g. fruits, berries (blueberries, raspberries), vegetables, coffee, tea, cacao, etc. Antioxidants can also be found in foods that are rich in Vitamin A C, E, and selenium that Brazil Nuts have a good proportion of. Therefore, it is essential to ensure that we

consume foods that have antioxidants throughout the dayto keep our energy levels. Drinking a cup of tea you like (green tea is excellent) Add lemon juice and a teaspoon of honey are refreshing drink.

9. Sweating - If the temperature is hot or humid and you're sweating often and are tired Put a small amount of salt from the sea (I always purchase Iodised) as well as a small amount of sugar, in a small amount of water and drink it down in an amount.

10. Energy Loss - If find yourself feeling less energetic or you are feeling anxious, take a minute to wash on your face and body with water. your energy will increase. Stop being seated to stretch your legs. Make sure you've had a meal lately (healthy foods). Do a sprint in the same spot for small amounts, such as at least 10 secs. Engage in something that's somewhat challenging to you, master an exercise routine, dance to some new music, solve crosswords, do puzzles, or other. This will all aid in the maintenance or increase of your energy levels. There

are, naturally products that you can purchase or that are included in to boost your energy levels, e.g. Guarana, Guarana B Vitamins as well as others. Doing research on these will provide good details on when and how to takethem if wanted to.

11. Power Nap Power Nap Power Naps boost brain power. If during the daytime, you are feeling tired (this is normal) then taking a Power Nap is wonderful.

A Power Nap can last between 20 and 30 minutes. (Set your alarm to 20 minutes when you must go somewhere else afterwards you have finished, so that there is no concern.) Use an eye-mask or protect your eyes by covering them with an eye mask so that it's dark (refer No.13 Below). If the noise is loud, but in a safe area, use earplugs. Lay on your back and be comfortably e.g. carpet or pillow if required. Then, place your hands (one over the other) upon your Solar Plexus. Make sure you keep your legs straight or uncrossed. Then, take a moment to rest (ensure that your thoughts are positive, if you're thinking).

Within 20 minutes your level of energy and mental performance will improve. If you get up, walk around a bit and drink a glass of water, and take a shower onto your face. You will feel more energetic. Even if you don't sleep or sleep for 15 minutes and still, your power nap will have given you energy to a extent. If you are unable to lie on your back , but can lie on your side it is likely that you would do it. You can then hold a cushion on the solar plexus.

12. Relaxation - Consciously and deliberately take time to unwind. Each of these can increase the hormones and chemicals that we require to be relaxed. But it's our thoughts that cause Stress. Stress drains the energy reservoir quickly and in a sneaky way. The chemical substances that our bodies produce during times of stress will make us believe that we have plenty of energy, but then we are exhausted, until we feel exhausted and

tired, but frequently unable to fall to sleep. I've heard that the chemical substances our bodies release to combat stress are more toxic to our bodies than any other poison known! We can manage short bursts of them however it is their continuous production that makes them harmful to us.

After overcoming the stress-related event when we are conscious of our breathing patterns and thoughts, we are able to make a decision to address these, i.e. shift our breathing from diaphragm to diaphragm, and turn negative thoughts into positive ones. It is therefore essential that we pay attention to the thoughts we think about and apply our extraordinary ability to alter them. Our body will cease creating the substances that eventually, make us exhausted and instead produce those that ease and make us feel relaxed and don't take our energy. So, we'll be more in coping when we're faced with at times.

If you are having trouble changing your thoughts. Find an area of ground or grass/earth, then take off your shoes. Walk in barefoot. This is known as Grounding. Also , a splash of cool drinking water in your skin can make a difference. Consume beverages or food that have antioxidants. This can help to re-energize your thinking process which will allow the positive energy to run in a new way.

13. Sleep - We are aware that it's important and the source of our energy, yet we have a hard time falling to sleep. I hope this article will assist in overcoming this.

It is believed that our Pineal Gland is very small but very strong. It produces the hormone Melatonin, which is needed for us to to sleep. The production begins as our eyes get dark during sleep, which is why it is essential to keep our eyes dark for a proper sleep. It releases it at its highest level at night, only from 11pm to 3am. It and then it slacks off until dawn. I've heard that at dawn the negative charge and the positive charge inside the Pineal Gland, touch and start to ignite, stopping the production of melatonin and infusing us with the day's intake of hormone Cortisol which started to release at 3am, when Melatonin began to decrease. Cortisol is created in the Adrenal Gland and is a huge help to deal with the pressure of the day that we are going through. Be aware to Research Cortisol before taking extra in the belief that you can do well with a lot of it! To be energetic, we are seeking the appropriate balance.

Melatonin is the hormone which informs the brain that it's time to go to sleep. It kicks in with dim lighting. It also acts as a scrubber of our brain, all dead cells, damaged tissue and all the waste that, if left it, could cause us to feel groggy at the beginning of the day, (and the rest of the day) and give the Free Radicals to get an ahead of the Antioxidants , and prevent the brain to discharge all the electrical charges and currents that our body needs to be in good health and function so that we are content and be able to cope in the stressful events that lie ahead. If this does not occur, we will eventually experience certain discomforts within our bodies, and eventually, we'll begin to notice a variety of malfunctions in our bodies. Below are some suggestions for how to make sure you sleep well.

Before bed If you're hungry, eat some carbohydrates such as Wholemeal (preservative no) toast, with something that's not sweet or a bowl muesli with very little sugar. At least 30 minutes prior to bedtime, switch off all lights off, shut all your computers away, take an ice-cold bath or shower (foot bathing using Epsom Salts is very beneficial). Once all the bathroom essentials are done, you can now relax in your bed.

Make sure you have a pen and pad close by and take note of the things you're looking to record. If you want, make observations inside your Journal or go through a book that soothes you and you're at the point where you can lie down.

We believe that sleeping means shutting down but it's an active time during which crucial processing, recovery and strengthening happens. The most potent healing hormones and chemicals can be released only when the eyes are shut. Wear an eye-mask when there is illumination in your sleep area. If it is cold, socks and a hot water bottle is ideal. If it is hot is the case, leave your feet away from the covers for a few minutes. Find a comfortable cushion to rest your head on, and add an extra cushion in between the legs of your feet to support your hips, and a tiny cushion to support your solar plexus until you fall the time you're asleep. Our head is now resting on the pillow. There are two options to help you fall asleep to sleep more easily.

The first step is to let yourself acknowledge that you are sleeping, after which you can accept that you're not asleep, acknowledge this and accept how you think about it regardless of the drama that you face in your day-to-day life. acknowledge that you are unable to change anything at the moment. Now, realize that right now, in this moment, that you're okay and it is safe to shut your eyes. It is safe to relax and be able to think positive thoughts, and to contemplate my thoughts and to become me.

The other is from my mother. You've done everything you need to do before you go to bed and you're lying asleep. Then, think about what you last did prior to getting in the bed (i.e. basic things such as brushing your teeth or whatever, but definitely not what others might are thinking about you and so on.) and then think of what you did before the event, before and prior to this. Now you're probably asleep , if not, you will you'll keep going back. this is known as "Un-Winding.". The next day, you might be amazed to find that you did not have to travel far back in the first place. It's also a great exercise to increase your mind's focus and mental memory.

If you've awakened slightly prior to the alarm sounding and you are tired, don't go to bed. A Power Nap earlier in the day, is more efficient for energy, so make plans for that. If you aren't ready to rise, lying on that Power Nap position can be enjoyable and an ideal time to boost positive thoughts.

2. Making Travelling Easier

1. Get Travel Insurance and know, in your policy exactly what you're protected from.

2. Try purchasing samples of your favorite products on the internet for small-sized travel toiletries for free or put moisturisers and shampoo into smaller containers with the quantities required. Make sure to write the content in the exterior. Note: If it is you find it difficult to write on your container, then put onto a strip of plaster, and then write down the contents using an ink pen that is waterproof.

3. Online bookings - Set up private browsing to prevent being detected by tracking systems, whereby they may be

more inclined to raise prices because you're considered to be a frequent user.

4. Flight Information - refer section 4 Apple Computer and Internet Tips No.17.

5. Certain areas seem to be more Static electricity around them. Placing a Dryer Sheet on in the lower part of your luggage will aid in reducing this and keeps your clothes fresh and clean.

6. Get rid of any containers for lotion or similar and place them as a beach bag to store your phone, money , and keys in separate containers, with the intention of keeping them safe on the beach. You can add a few bread clips to the other in case your thong strap fails as well as a bag to hold all rubbish collections, be it or any other. Include a tent peg so that you can put it on the ground, allowing you to stop or deter the bag from being taken by a burglar.

7. A small bag that is tied to you waist (thin bum bag) can be useful for storing your passport or mobile phone, a card with ID contact information on the back, a

tissue, small pencil and paper, and some cash.

8. Conserve space by rolling towels, clothes and other items and putting socks and underwear inside your shoes. Glass cases are ideal for storing phone and computer cables and chargers jewelry, cables, etc.

9. The collars of shirts can be lined with belts to keep tidy. A small hair blow-dryer with a splash of water, is a great way to remove wrinkles from clothing. A bulldog or binder clip can be used to shield the razor's head and can also be used to secure wound-up cords for headphones to stop them from getting caught in a knot. Tic Containers for Tac are useful to keep the safety pins and hair clip. A small soap cake in a washcloth, with a light weight, is useful for freshening ourselves up (put inside a zip top bag, so there is no need to worry if it gets the soap is damp).

A light-weight towel can be useful to dry clothes that have been washed lightly - wash your item, wrap it in the towel, wring it tight or dance/stomp it. This gives you a greater chances of drying faster and it will keep the light towel for a longer time is also helpful.

10. In your bag on the plane The following is the recommended order to pack small quantities with Baby Wipes, great for underarm hygiene and for women some Pantie Liners in the case that your main luggage gets lost or you need to extend the wearing your underwear. Take a head scarf that you can serve as a hair band in the event that our hair gets messy (different climates can affect the condition of our hair and skin quickly). Keep a small amount of moisturiser inside your bag since different conditions and climates can cause dryness to our noses and skin.

A chewing gum piece can be handy for when your ears begin to hurt after the flight. You should chew it well and then drop your jaw. It is possible to take a couple of Strepsil or similar lozenges to ensure fresh breath and to ward off any new bacteria. Take note that for the test of breath freshness take a lick of your wrist and sniff it. The smell will inform you whether you should act. If you have a persistent bad breath, put taking a small amount of Apple Cider Vinegar in some water, and then take a swallow or spit out as you wish (can add honey if you want).

Tweezers, nail clippers, file along with a few bacteria-friendly wipes and some plaster strips, a tiny pair of scissors is handy (check for if they are allowed) A small blow up pillow , and an assortment of cards could be helpful if a delay in your flight, particularly in the event that you have children travelling on board and the mobile phone batteries are dead. A lightweight wrap can be useful in this situation because waiting in airports can get very cold.

Tablets for water purification are necessary when bottled water is not readily available at your location. Dental floss (non waxed) can be useful in the event that you have to tie something and, of course, to floss your teeth. A plastic bag to store rubbish or any other purpose that might arise or arise. A spare pair of socks or stockings as well as a brush and pen, of course, and. A plastic water bottle that is empty can be useful if you've passed by security (where water bottles is not permitted to be used) and you want to refill it later with water instead of buying water in the event that you are delayed on your trip.

11. Write on a card your name as well as the name of your Home Country, Emergency contact details, the name of your next of kin blood type, and your telephone number for your accommodation or contact number. Photograph copies of all your documents and cards. place the photocopies in the waterproof clip bag. keep it apart from the actual items. Keep a bit of cash in a smaller container to use in an emergency only.

12. Request an indestructible Sticker when you check in if you have concerns about your luggage getting damaged. This can

also improve the likelihood of your luggage getting off the conveyor belt first.

13. The feeling of travel sickness (Nausea) You can tilt your head either way. Breathing in a diaphragm with awareness. In your wrist, put the tips of your three fingers in between two of the tendons. Flex your legs and turn the ankles, then move your the neck a bit. Make sure to splash the face and neck with water. sip some and walk around a bit in case you're it is possible. Be sure to are carrying a plastic bag which takes away the stress of "what if I vomit in the bathroom', thereby helping to calm down and is, of course, it is necessary in the event that you have to.

14. Check at ATMs or Cash Machines what the exchange rate local to you is since it may not have the fees other Money Converters typically charge.

15. Photograph yourself and your family before you leave your hotel throughout the day (in the event of an incident, this is the best picture you could give an officer from the Police). Always set up a meeting

place and time with anyone you travel with you, in case you're separated. Always bring along the address and name of your accommodation (write it on your arm, too!). You should only stay in areas classified as safe.

16. If you're looking for directions to a town that is not yours the best option is to go to the Fast Food Outlet that has an delivery service.

17. Utilize Google Maps offline by typing "OK Maps" and the location that you are within will be stored for future usage if required.

18. If you've lost or are unable to locate your laptop or smartphone's on the wall You can charge your devices through the USB port on many modern televisions.

19. I love freshly-made Chips/French Fries as opposed which have been prepared for a long time (and usually, they are excessively salted). If you're like me and want to have them without salt, ask for unseasoned Fries They will usually, make fresh batches for you. Then, you can salt

them following your preferred quantity of salt.

20. If you are in an elevator and notice that all the buttons have been in use but there is no one else is in the elevator, pressing each button two times is a great chance that it will not stop on each floor.

3. YouTube Gems

1. Are you worried about what your children can access the internet? YouTube In contrast to the normal YouTube, Google built the kid version with filters that stop any content that may be considered to be unsafe content suitable for children. The app is known as YouTube Kids and it's free. Parents can install the app onto your child's smartphone (compatible for Android and iOS) and create other restrictions including limit screen time, setting a limit on the volume, and removing comments.

2. To obtain the transcript of the entire video, click the button'more' (at the lower right on the screen) and a drop-down menu will be displayed. Select 'Transcript'.

Note : If you don't see any indication that it has been previously programmed to be hidden from view.

3. To download a YouTube video - add'ss' to the URL that is between www. and youtube.com.

Example: www.ssyoutube.com. You will need to download the application they request you to. There are many YouTube video downloaders available on the internet for you to select from.

4. In between, type'repeat' www.youtube or .com to play the desired video in a sequence.

Example: www.youtuberepeat.com

5. To view YouTube's age-restricted videos without signing up you must add 'nsfw' to 'youtube.com'.

Example: www.nsfwyoutube.com

6. To watch a YouTube video in TV Mode - Type in - Youtube.com/leanback.

7. If you're watching a video from YouTube and you'd like to have a slow motion, hold

the space bar to the left. If you're looking for a higher high-quality slow motion join the YouTube HTML five Video Player.

8. To skip over a video, 5 seconds forward and back use the arrow keys: both left and right.

To skip a video for 10 seconds forward and backward Press J to go the back, as well as L to go forward.

9. Utilize your numbers keypad (123456789) to scroll through videos faster than using the Arrow keys.

10. By pressing K at your keyboard can stop the YouTube video.

4. Tips for Apple Computers and Internet

Apple Computer:

Here are some shortcuts I've found useful in documents:

To do Use

1. To create a new folder, press Shift - Command-N

For creating Document SettingsShift-command-P

2. To open the Spelling as well as Grammar window, press Shift - Command -

3. Then delete the characters on the left

Then delete all characters that are to the left- - fn - - delete

4. To get directly to the beginning the command is up the arrow

To get straight to the finish line, type down the arrow

5. To scroll upwards to the beginning Fn Left to right

To scroll to the bottom -Fn Right Arrow

6. To scroll down a page, use fn - Down Arrow

To scroll one page up -- - fn arrow up

7. To return from the end of the paragraphControl A

To get to the conclusion of the paragraph control E

8. To get to the start of your line, the command left to go to the beginning of your line

To reach the end of the line- - command right left

Internet Tips:

9. When you visit an Internet page On a website, you will see that the Space bar scrolls downwards and, when you press the shift key, and then press the Space bar, it will scroll upwards.

10. Do not close the browser tab by accident - On Apple computers, simply click the option "Window" on the right side of your screen . then select the 'Pin Tab This will shut off the possibility of closing the webpage that you do not wish to close.

For computers running Windows - Right Click on the Tab that you don't wish to close, and then select the 'Pin' Tab option. When you wish to close the "Pinned Tab or Pin Tab' on any type of computer, return to the menu and choose "Unpin Tab'.

11. A PDF File download If it is ending with '.exe It is a virus, remove it right away.

12. FourSquare.com is a fantastic website to find great restaurants as well as WiFi passwords. On FourSquare enter the address where you're located and then check the comment section to find WiFi passwords.

13. In the Netflix show If you would like to find out which name is used for the Song and the Artist playing you can turn on 'Closed Captioning to display the information. be displayed.

14. Today, we don't have to enter www. before looking for a website.

Google has a lot to offer users of its search engine. Take advantage of the following tips, Tricks and Hacks to improve your experience on the internet that bit simpler.

15. Google to find the lyrics of a song or a quote, phrase or a proverb , but you're not

able to recall all the words needed to locate it. Use an Asterisk (*) for every word that you are unable to remember. For instance of the song "Love is in the air'. You've always thought of it as "Love was on the Air and you're aware that's not the case. Type in your search"Love * in the Air It will show "Love is in the Air'. If you typed "Love in the Air", you will receive everything connected to Love in the Air.

16. On Google If you're looking for a solution to a computer issue Add'solved' your search query. It appears to locate the answer faster than the normal time .

17. Are you looking to know your flight's status? Just enter your airline's name and flight number into Google's search bar, and Google will give you an overview of your flight's present situation. It is only applicable for flights departing or arriving within the next 24hrs.

18. Don't have a timer on hand - Type in Googles search bar - Set timer for your desired seconds/minutes/hours - Google will bring one up for you. Google also

provides the capability of setting alarms. For instance, if it's 11am and you'd like to set your alarm to 11:30am. just type in the timer to 11:30, and Google will show the correct timer to set an alarm to sound at this point. There's also an option to set a stop watch also.

19. Undecided about something? Enter Googles search bar and flip a coin and Google will flip the coin on your behalf.

20. Do you want to roll a dice but don't have a die? Enter Google's search bar and roll a die Google will roll the die for you.

21. Are you unsure of the amount you should tip an individual or business you know? Type it into Googles search bar, Tipping then the total amount that you paid for the total. If, for example, you paid $20 for a meal, you can type 'tip 20$ then select the amount you'd like to pay.

22. Do you want to make your Google search results? Try these entertaining tricks.

Enter "Google Sphere and click on the first result (Mr.doob) and witness the magic unfold.

Google Gravity', click the first results (Mr.doob) and you will see your search bar fall to the ground! These two tricks are fantastic to impress your friends with because the trick won't begin until you've moved your mouse.

23. Need to relax and get away from work? Take a look at the games Google offers.

In the search bar, type 'Atari Breakout' Googles search bar, and then enjoy some fun playing Googles Atari game.

Enter 'Google Pac-man' into Google's search bar. Take some time out to play Googles Pac-man game.

24. Do a barrel roll" in Googles search bar, then click on the first result (Do the barrel roll, Elope) and then watch your website make an actual barrel roll!

5. Improving Your Health

1. Sunburn and minor Burns Relief - First, make sure to avoid sunburn. Aloe Vera plant sap works well and is able to be frozen in ice cube tray.

I am disgusted by the preservatives that are in many sunscreens. I noticed this after my face was burned by it (which was different from the sun's burning) which is why I now apply to my skin a small amount of un-refined Olive Oil. On www.globalhealingcentre.com on the benefits of Olive Oil states this oil protects against ultraviolet rays and has good proponents for our skin. I've never had any burns with this oil, and I have found it beneficial to my face.

If you plan to stay in the sun, ensure that you are adequately protecting yourself, including the long sleeves (lose cotton fabric is good) or a cap with a hat that covers your face, etc.

2. Burnt Tongue - Put a small amount of sweet white sugar directly on the area, where it is burned and allow it to dissolve. Let it sit for about a minute, and then you

will feel the pain diminish after which you can spit it out and wash your mouth out with water. Do not drink or consume any food with acidic ingredients until your tongue is feeling normal.

3. Tight or Sore Throat Add a teaspoon of Sea Salt in a little warm water and gargle it. Spit it out, repeating three times to ease the pain. Another option is to put 1 spoonful of Apple Cider Vinegar in a tiny amount of water (with some honey, if desired as Honey helps to moisten the throat) Gargle, then swallow it.

An elderly lady friend suggests that an L-Lysine (with no added ingredients) tablet can be a great product to maintain her. A strepsil, also known as a lozenge, will naturally ease your throat.

4. Eyes - If your eyes are get irritated or you notice that you're scratching one or both then you might have an eyelash curled that is irritating your eyes. Utilizing a careful, use tweezers with clean edges to pull out a few eyelashes near the corners of your eyes . examine if you feel relief. If

your eye is scratched, it may take a few days and then a little time to heal. minimal discomfort, but you'll feel the change.

After you've done your work close (computer screens) Take 30 seconds to focus on the farthest thing you could see. This can help a lot to return your vision back to normal.

5. Ears - Swimmers' Ear (water/moisture within the ear canal that can irritate the ear lining) (irritating lining of the ear canal) Otocomb Ear Ointment (prescription from the doctor) is a solution one of my friends suggested works. Blue Tac can be used to block your ear's entrance bathing, showering and so on. This is a great way to prevent irritation in the future.

Ears Blocked If my ears appear to be blocked by wax, I go for a dip in the ocean. It has worked great for my ears. You could also visit your Doctor and ask them to cleanse your ears using a specific kind of syringe. This is the most effective method for getting rid of a build-up of wax, but it could require a fee from your doctor. It is important to note that blocked ears can result in Sinus problems as well.

Audiologists (Ear Specialists) have reported that playing music that is too loud while using earphones, could cause irreparable loss of hearing.

6. Nausea - Stomach upset Try eating a slice of bread (with no preservatives). Remember what you ate and take the appropriate action in accordance with the degree of discomfort.

For Wind - drink an ounce of hot or warm (tea hot) water or a small amount of Soda water. Massage your stomach in a circular motion, or gently apply pressure using two fingers on your solar plexus and hold it for one minute. Take a walk around. Be aware that if you awake with wind-related pain, first you'll want to work by relieving the pain, and then you should remember if you've consumed something that was different from the usual (it might be a different brand that you purchased this time, or something you've that was not eaten for a while or even a while.) in order to prevent the possibility of suffering in the future. Consult your doctor if the best way to avoid future pain.

7. Body Balance - Workout as well as use your more frequently used hand to help maintain balance e.g. brushing your teeth, hair cleaning up trash, etc. Be sure to check that your knees are not bent when you are standing and walking.

Walking on a low ground plank, arms extended, is a good idea but don't pull yourself up a flight of stairs (use rail as a guide and support, but don't lift yourself up unless you are in an emergency situation).

I believe that headstands, if started in the early years and continue to help us maintain our balance and keep our circulatory system in good shape when we get older, but consult your doctor whether you're not 'young' anymore prior to doing. Be sure that the area around you is clean. Put a cushion on your head, and then use the wall to support your feet.

8. Exercise regularly - Regular exercise is very beneficial to human beings. Do it. Even if it's things that aren't too big, like taking a walk or running in the street for just a minute. Every single exercise is beneficial to our health, so if you're not doing any exercise begin small. when you begin to feel the benefits and begin to feel the benefits, you'll likely be motivated to keep doing it and more more.

9. Dry or burned lips chapsticks and other general moisturisers that have no preservatives, and olive oil are great for me. However, if you have there is nothing in your cupboard, go with the traditional method that is to rub along the exterior of your nose using your fingers and then wipe your lips. It might seem odd, but the exterior of your nose is awash with the perfect oil to nourish you lips. So try it. The act of licking your lips by licking them with your tongue can make them dry, but it's an excellent sign that you need to moisturize them immediately.

10. Hair cutting with sharp scissors makes a big impact!

11. Feeling dizzy ? Take your breath (by diaphragm that is expanding) and then place your hand on something that is stable. This will enable your brain to calm down from the confusion that is often experienced when being dizzy. It will also help you feel more stable. This will allow you to feel more secure to take the appropriate actions.

12. A mild headache - squeeze downwards on the webbed portion of your palm between your thumb and index finger. Do this for about 4 minutes. Then take a glass or two of water. The headache will ease.

13. Mobile Phone - Don't put your mobile phone on your ear if it's got 10 percent or less capacity (the electromagnetic radiation is measured at 1000 times higher than a fully charged battery).

14. Homemade Cold Pack Purchase a small sauce packet from the Fish & Chips shop or Bakery and then freeze it. These are great for little bumps that occur on fingers

and toes, lips nose etc. They are able to wrap around them.

15. Acne and Scars Acne and scars - Apply a tiny amount of honey (recommend organic) on the area affected like you would apply a face Mask Relax or lay on your back, and then put on a few of your favourite music on i.e. take a break for a while, and then wash it off. Be aware that the product "Wound Gel is a honey-based product that you can use to soothe it, and may not be as sticky to be used. Additionally, it has been reported that the Head and Shoulders Shampoo is a product that has pyrithione has been proven to help clear the appearance of Acne on the back, face, and chest. I loved Proactive (on the internet) to clear acne.

Always wash your hands before you go to bed because often we rest the hands of our cheeks while we sleep, and can transmit bacteria, if there is any. Also often wash the covers of your pillows in the same way.

16. Weight loss - Eat a nutritious breakfast with protein, but does not contain fat. In the afternoon, eat regular health-giving food items throughout the day. Be aware that when we don't consume food for 12 hours the metabolism slows by 40 percent. It is therefore more beneficial to eat frequently but not in large quantities and at the same time. Reduce the amount of salt and sugar to a minimal levels, drink plenty water, do some exercises and stretches , and focus on positive thoughts only. Eliminate alcohol, or drink just a small amount if you need to you to do so. Everyday, you should look in the mirror and tell yourself that you're beautiful and attractive and then believe in it. You will see your body's image change instantly. The local Gym will guide you to the most effective exercises to do for your body. Always talk about your weight with your doctor.

17. Water Tips I've noted one glass prior to a shower can help to lower your blood pressure. A glass of water 30 minutes before eating meals will aid in your

digestion. Two glasses following awaking can help stimulate your internal organs and one glass prior to going to bed can help keep you from having a stroke or heart attack, even though there is a possibility that you will wake up needing to go to the bathroom. But, if I had any signs of these illnesses I would be able to tolerate it, and I would also be able to consult my doctor in case of any concern.

18. Get rid of dead skin cells Dead cells peel off at all times and block our pores. There are a variety of high-quality products available like exfoliating gloves, exfoliating creams. And in nature there is Beach sand which can be applied gently. Note - Recommend moisturising your skin after exfoliating it.

19. The Drug "ICE" - Prior to signing a contract to move into a new property, you must purchase a the ICE Test Kit (around $ 100) and check the interior part of the structure. The 'ICE' remains in the ceiling fans, walls , and so on. After all has gone away and is known to cause serious health

problems and cost you an enormous amount of money to wash it out of it.

20. Mold If you've had the experience of having Mold in your system , the product NeilMed Sinus Wash (Chemist like product) is sure to be a welcome to you. I've known of someone who has been infected with an extensive 'burst' Mold poisoning following a visit to an old, damp building. I have witnessed how debilitating this affected the patient who was unable to return to normal before the use of NeilMed Sinus Rinse.

To eliminate small areas of Mold within the home (often in drains) If you'd prefer not to employ Bleach Then Clove Oil, few drops in water, spray the area before spraying it down the drains. After a thorough spray into the drain, place the plug in and let it sit for a few hours before taking the water out.

21. Restless Legs Syndrome - If you are taking medication, consult your doctor first. If not you can take a teaspoon of Apple Cider Vinegar mixed with some

water, then add honey if you desire, and then take the recommended dose. Take note that if you drink excessive amounts of cider vinegar in one day, you'll get a taste afterward, so reduce the dosage.

22. Self-Defense - Learning the best self-defense moves is an excellent method of exercising and can boost your self-esteem and could come in extremely handy in the event of anyone attempt to harm you. There are a variety of forms available of self-defence, so choose one that works for you. The majority of gyms offer classes on self-defense and will be happy to provide information and talk about your goals. It is still important to make use of our common sense and avoid dangerous situations when we are aware of them However, learning self-defence can help in many other areas like building muscles, establishing a proper posture, and improving stance just to mention just a few.

6. Tips for Cars

1. You've lost the location you left your car in This is only available for electronic keys. Set yourself in the range of where you believe you might find it. You can either take your key and put it on your head. Alternatively place your water bottle over your head and place your key at it. Each of them will extend the range that your key will be able to operate, causing the car to sound when it is opened.

2. Smartphone Holder Insert a quality rubber band into the air con vent in order to make an inexpensive holder. Be aware that it is inside the band, your phone will not be used.

3. Cool the interior of a car that is very hot. You can roll down one of the windows completely, and then walk to the opposite side of the car , and shut and open that door several times. This will let much of your hot air away of the car in only a couple of minutes.

4. Small scratches - Try applying clear nail polish over the scratch.

5. Low-cost Car Air Freshener - An open container of Dryer Sheets inside your car provides an excellent scent and can keep you entertained for a long time. A sealed bag of Fabric Softener at the rear of your car provides a pleasant scent and lasts for longer.

6. Steering Wheel - If it is the day that is hot, cover the steering wheel of your vehicle with towels.

7. Filling your tank with fuel - hold the trigger for a few seconds to prevent getting too much gas in your tank Many people believe that you will also gain more fuel from your money when you do this.

8. The headlights may be hazy. Use toothpaste to cleanse them It's a great solution.

9. Blacken tyres using Cola mixed with detergent and then applied and then rinsed off. It works great.

10. Items for shopping and rubbish A laundry basket at the rear of your vehicle to bring in all your shopping bags at the

same time. A small container in the back of the car can be handy for keeping trash in order and to make the garbage disposal to be made easier.

11. Pouring oil - When you have to pour oil into your vehicle but do not have a funnel in your vehicle Place a screw driver or something similar to it, at the area the place you'd like the oil to flow. The oil is sprayed over the screwdriver.

If you keep doing this in a steady and slow manner it will work.

7. When In The Wilderness

1. Food amounts - Transfer food items such as spices and herbs to an old and clean Tic Tac container or similar. Be sure to note with a waterproof marker pen the exact contents on the container.

2. Chalk is handy to keep to have on hand in the event you get lost, or to mark the trees to track your route and to avoid walking around since it's common.

3. Light Raincoat - Place an enormous garbage bag inside your gear so that, in

the event that it rains, and you need to protect yourself, you could cut an opening for your arms and head.

4. Candle wick lighting - pack in a few strands of dried spaghetti sticks. Use the light at the end of one, and then use it to ignite your candle once the candle is empty in its container.

5. Fire / Kindling - Corn Chips similar to Doritos are great in the absence of dry kindling. A crayon in your equipment can be useful since they last for about 30 minutes on average.

6. Drying out Equipment to have a greater chance of keeping toilet paper in good condition, choose the appropriate screw lid container made of plastic that is slightly larger than your toilet paper. Cut a suitable cut in one side, and then place the toilet roll in it and feed it through the cut.

Make sure to keep all documents on paper or anything that is not waterproof , in a screw-top container. Items like rice beans, flour, beans and similar items should be kept in bottles or plastic containers instead of bags in order to remain watertight.

A thin drop Sheet (which is available at a discount type shop usually, for a low price) It is useful when it rains. It is possible to line your bag, place it into your bag, and attach the drop sheet to close the top.

7. Dry cheese Dry - Smear a bit of butter on it, then seal it in an airtight container.

8. Avoiding bugs - Use the bright torch or flashlight. It should be placed a bit away from the campsite and tilt it upwards to the sky. The insects will be attracted to the light, and you'll be bothered much less by insects.

While sleeping, put on headphones or an earband around your head, in order to prevent a bug from entering your ear (it is terrifying). If it does happen, you can use the torch or similar light and tilt your head to ensure that it is facing your upper side , and reflect the light or torch over the ear's entrance. typically, the bug will crawl and then back to the Light! Best I can do. It's worked, but I cannot be guaranteed when it comes to bugs.

Always carry a small container of insect spray as insects have different breading times and it's not uncommon for them to see a swarm appear and, in this case, you'll need to spray your camping site or tent. In other words, they're everywhere and will stay until they go to the grave!

9. Bug Eliminating - Add a teaspoon of Vanilla Extract to a small amount of water, then dab your body with the extract. I applied vanilla essence Imitation (in small amounts of amount of water) and dabbed it all over my legs, arms and a bit on my back neck. I wasn't at all bothered for an hour . That was enough for me and could have reapplied it when I wanted to keep it more.

A friend of mine makes Soya Wax candles , and then adds Vanilla (scent) into it. She says that burning the candles keeps Mossies away. Incredibly, I've studied studies using Soybean Oil (the kind that you can cook with) and they found that, products that contain Soybean oil helped keep mosquitoes at bay for 94.6 minutes, which is more than any other repellent derived from plants which was examined. Additionally, lemon Eucalyptus oil, which is 40 percent in some waters is another natural repellent. The scent is more appealing than the coils that burn that you purchase from the store.

For Spiders To repel spiders, use a bit of white vinegar mixed with water inside a spray bottle. Spray your tent in the outside area if you're worried about the spiders.

10. Itchy Insect or Mosquito Bites - Place an extremely heated (standard temperature) spoon over the bite. The heat will kill the protein responsible for the itching. Another option is to make a circle around the bite with a finger nail clean, and then criss-cross the bite using that same finger nail.

A friend was badly bit with Midgies The itching became horrible and the bites appeared to be red and inflamed. In desperate circumstances, he put Iodised

Sea Salt on a damp cloth and applied it on the bites. He reported that it hurt for a short time, but it was more pleasant than itching, the stinging stopped and there was no itch . The bites healed very quickly.

11. Tick Bites - Keep some Methylated Spirits on hand. Do a dab or tip a small bit of the tick and then leave it for five minutes. It'll paralyze it and decrease the grip it has. then, using tweezers, put it beneath the tick. Then, as I've experienced the entire tick is easily is removed.

12. Asthma and/or Allergy Symptoms Take a few bottles of apple cider vinegar in your the go. If you, or someone else is running out of the usual method of treating the issue and you require relief, you can put at least a teaspoon of Apple Cider Vinegar in some water and drink. It is believed to work , but should you have any doubts, always seek medical advice as needed.

8. Amazing Hacks for the Kitchen and Around the Home

1. Reading Glasses Steam can reduce vision Spit them on and spread it on the

glass using your fingers and rinse them under water. allow to dry (or dab and not wipe dry them) and it will help tons. Also, this applies to snorkel and swimming goggles (spit and spread it out, then rinse with seawater). There are other products available to accomplish this. The act of spitting on them is an individual issue. Always wash your hands afterward, especially when you are handling food in particular.

2. Expand counter space by pulling your drawers out and put an edging board on the top.

3. Hangers for Skirts and Pants (the ones with clips) are ideal to open a book.

4. Hygiene After handling food items from your Cook Book or the Menu in a restaurant, clean your hands prior to actual food handling. Hair should be tied up while cooking to ensure that you don't lose your hair while eating.

5. Cooking Ingredients You can use a muffin tray to arrange in order, if you wish each of the smaller ingredients required

for cooking your recipe, making it simple to add. Note : Kids like doing this, and it's a great opportunity to involve them.

6. Stop the water from boiling - Set a wooden spoon in the pot that is boiling.

7. Shelling Eggs Boiled - If are having trouble or have lots to accomplish, then include half an teaspoon baking Soda in the water so that the shells break off more easily.

8. Sour cream and cottage cheese Last longer when the container is turned upside down in the fridge. I've heard it helps to prevent the growth of bacteria.

9. Freezed Pizza and heating food Slice the pizza prior to cooking it or placing in the in the microwave. It's easy to cut when frozen, and you don't have the sensation of moving the toppings around! If you are reheating food, an outline of a small circle around it. This gives more heat distribution and avoid the food from becoming cold in the centre.

10. Save power (and wash-up) when cooking rice, cook for 10 minutes until it's cooked Add any quick cooking green e.g. spinach leaves, broccoli , etc.

11. Mixture that spills out within the Microwave If the mix has dried out, you can put the vinegar in the water and microwave for up to 4 minutes. It will cause it to loosen after which a quick wipe off is all that's required.

12. Cooling Water To keep your drink cooler or whatever you'd like to cool faster put it inside damp or soiled paper (Paper Towels good) and put it in the freezer or fridge. For gorgeous cold water to drink, just fill up your water bottle with one third and put it inside your freezer on the side. Later once it's frozen and is needed take it out of the freezer and add regular cold water to fill it up.

Conclusion

Life is stressful enough. There are ways to ease your stress by being more creative and ingenuous. There is no need to be an expert on everything, nor do you necessarily need to have the answer to every problem. The only thing you need to do is try to ease your stress by using life hacks.

Life hacks are easy solutions to the everyday issues. These life hacks can help you live your life more easily. They will help you deal with difficult situations without anxiety and stress. If you're at home or at work it is possible to use these hacks to be an efficient and reliable individual.

Life hacks let you utilize things for other purposes beyond what they were originally designed to serve. In a way life hacks allow you to accomplish things more efficiently simply by being ingenuous and imaginative. The more creative and creative you can be, the more efficient your life will become.

Life hacks don't have to be costly. In fact, what you need could be at hand.

In your home, you can make use of life hacks to complete your chores at home. They are particularly helpful when doing chores such as cleaning the home or washing laundry. Life hacks can be extremely helpful for keeping everything running smoothly within your home.

At work In your workplace, you can utilize techniques to be a efficient employee. These life hacks will enable you to finish your job quicker and more efficiently. This will make you more efficient. You will be a better worker in the event that you know what hacks you can use.

While traveling on a trip, you can utilize different life hacks. They can prevent you from having problems when you travel to the foreign country. They also permit you to save a substantial amount of cash. Life hacks can give you the most practical and economical way to spend your trips.

If you believe you've got a weak memory, life hacks may assist you! Simply

www.ingramcontent.com/pod-product-compliance
Lightning Source LLC
Chambersburg PA
CBHW050405120526
44590CB00015B/1837